Opinions and Lifestyle Survey - 2023 Supplement

Contents

3301235712

Statistical bulletin

Public opinions and social trends, Great Britain: 20 September to 1 October 2023

Social insights on daily life and events, including estimates from the Opinions and Lifestyle Survey (OPN) relating to the biggest issues facing society today.

Contact:
Laura Fairey, Jodie Davis and Tim Vizard
policy.evidence.analysis@ons. gov.uk
+44 3000 671543

Release date:
6 October 2023

Next release:
20 October 2023

Table of contents

1 . Main Points

The following information is for the latest survey period 20 September to 1 October 2023, based on adults in Great Britain.

- When asked about the important issues facing the UK today, the most commonly reported issues continued to be the cost of living (90%), the NHS (86%), the economy (72%), climate change and the environment (62%) and housing (58%).

- More than half (54%) of adults reported that their cost of living had increased compared with a month ago, while 44% reported it had stayed the same and 2% said it had decreased.

- More than 9 in 10 (94%) adults who reported their cost of living had increased compared to one month ago reported the price of their food shop had increased, 65% reported the price of their fuel had increased and 58% reported their gas or electricity bills had increased.

- When asked about what people are doing because of the increases in the cost of living, 65% said they were spending less on non-essentials, around half of all adults (48%) were shopping around more, 47% of adults were using less fuel such as gas or electricity in their homes, and more than 4 in 10 (44%) were spending less on food shopping and essentials.

- Among those currently paying rent or a mortgage, almost a half (47%) of adults reported that their rent or mortgage payments had gone up in the past 6 months; this has increased from 33% during a similar period one year ago (29 September to 9 October 2022).

- Among those who are currently paying rent or a mortgage, 40% reported finding it very or somewhat difficult affording these payments; this is up from 30% during a similar period one year ago (29 September to 9 October 2022).

- Of those who pay energy bills, around 4 in 10 (43%) adults reported it being very or somewhat difficult to afford energy bills; this is the same as in a similar period last year (29 September to 9 October 2022).

2 . Public opinions and social trends data

Public opinions and social trends, Great Britain: household finances
Dataset | Released 6 October 2023
Indicators from the Opinions and Lifestyle Survey (OPN) of people's experiences of changes in their cost of living and household finances in Great Britain.

Public opinions and social trends, Great Britain: personal well-being and loneliness
Dataset | Released 6 October 2023
Indicators from the Opinions and Lifestyle Survey (OPN) of worries, personal well-being, and loneliness in Great Britain.

Public opinions and social trends, Great Britain: personal experiences of shortages of goods
Dataset | Released 6 October 2023
Indicators from the Opinions and Lifestyle Survey (OPN) of whether people experienced shortages of goods such as food, medicine, or fuel when shopping in Great Britain.

Public opinions and social trends, Great Britain: GP practice access
Dataset | Released 6 October 2023
Indicators from the Opinions and Lifestyle Survey (OPN) related to people's experiences of GP practice access in Great Britain.

3 . Measuring the data

This release contains data and indicators from the Office for National Statistics' (ONS's) Opinions and Lifestyle Survey (OPN).

From the 16 June 2023 release onwards, we have made changes that reduce the scope of the release and accompanying datasets. This is based on a routine review of the relevance and usefulness of this release.

Breakdowns by age and sex are no longer provided for fortnightly estimates in the latest Public opinions and social trends, Great Britain datasets. All previous versions of the dataset remain available from this page. Estimates from the OPN by these and other personal characteristics will continue to be provided on a regular basis in other ONS releases. For example, OPN estimates relating to the impact of cost of living among different sub-groups of the population are provided within the regular Impact of increased cost of living on adults across Great Britain series.

Confidence intervals are provided for all estimates in the datasets. Where changes in results from previous weeks are presented in this release, or comparisons between estimates are made, associated confidence intervals should be used to assess the statistical significance of the differences.

Sampling and weighting

In the latest period (20 September to 1 October 2023), we sampled 4,963 households. This sample was randomly selected from people who had previously completed the Labour Market Survey (LMS) or OPN. The responding sample for the latest period contained 2,364 individuals, representing a 47.6% response rate.

Survey weights were applied to make estimates representative of the population (based on ONS population estimates). Further information on the survey design and quality can be found in our Opinions and Lifestyle Survey Quality and Methodology Information (QMI).

4 . Related links

Student voices: experiences of the rising cost of living
Article | Released 6 September 2023
The rising cost of living has brought new challenges to higher education, with student budgets being squeezed. Interviews with students in England during the 2022 to 2023 academic year have helped shed light on the difficulties they are facing.

Climate change insights, families and households, UK: August 2023
Article | Released 11 August 2023
Latest climate change-related analysis using a range of UK official statistics.

UK Measures of National Well-being: August 2023
Article | Released 11 August 2023
An update on the UK's progress across ten domains of national well-being which include personal well-being, relationships, health, what we do, where we live, personal finance, economy, education and skills, governance, and the environment.

Impact of increased cost of living on adults across Great Britain: February to May 2023
Article | Released 14 July 2023
Analysis of the proportion of the population that are affected by an increase in their cost of living, and of the characteristics associated with financial vulnerability, using data from the Opinions and Lifestyle survey.

Understanding AI uptake and sentiment among people and businesses in the UK
Article | Released 16 June 2023
An exploration into the use of Artificial Intelligence (AI) and how people feel about its uptake in today's society and business.

Tracking the impact of winter pressures in Great Britain: November 2022 to February 2023
Article | Released 24 April 2023
Insights from our Winter Survey as we tracked participants to examine how increases in the cost of living and difficulty accessing NHS services had impacted their lives during the winter months.

Cost of living insights
Web page | Updated frequently
The latest data and trends about the cost of living. Explore changes in the cost of everyday items and how this is affecting people.

5 . Cite this statistical bulletin

Office for National Statistics (ONS), released 6 October 2023, ONS website, statistical bulletin, Public opinions and social trends, Great Britain: 20 September to 1 October 2023

Office for
National Statistics

Data and analysis from Census 2021

Impact of increased cost of living on adults across Great Britain: June to September 2022

Analysis of the proportion of the population that are affected by an increase in their cost of living, and of the characteristics associated with having difficulty affording or being behind on energy, mortgage or rental payments, using data from the Opinions and Lifestyle Survey.

Contact:
Caleb Ogwuru, Laura Fairey, David Ainslie and Tim Vizard

Release date:
25 October 2022

Correction

17 February 2023 10:00

We have corrected an issue affecting some of the estimates published in Figure 12. This is because of a weighting error which resulted in Wales and Scotland being weighted to the wrong populations. This issue occurred because of a processing error and should not impact any future analysis. This error does not affect the message or findings. We apologise for any inconvenience caused.

Table of contents

1. Main points

The experiences of different groups of the population in having difficulty affording or being behind on their energy, rent or mortgage payments, in the period 22 June to 11 September 2022, have been examined using the Opinions and Lifestyle Survey (OPN).

- The proportion of all adults finding it difficult (very or somewhat) to afford their energy bills, rent or mortgage payments has increased through the year, almost half of adults (45%) who paid energy bills (40% in March to June 2022) and 30% paying rent or mortgages reported these being difficult to afford (26% March to June 2022).

- Over half (55%) of disabled adults reported finding it difficult to afford their energy bills, and around a third (36%) found it difficult to afford their rent or mortgage payments compared with 40% and 27% of non-disabled people, respectively.

- Around 4 in 10 (44%) White adults reported finding it difficult to afford their energy bills, compared with around two-thirds (69%) for Black or Black British adults and around 6 in 10 (59%) Asian or Asian British adults.

- Around 6 in 10 (60%) renters reported finding it difficult to afford their energy bills, and around 4 in 10 (39%) found it difficult to afford their rent payments compared with 43% and 23% of those with a mortgage, respectively.

- Around half of those with a personal income of less than £20,000 per year said they found it difficult to afford their energy bills; this proportion decreased as personal income increased, with around a quarter (23%) of those earning £50,000 or more reporting this.

- In the period 29 September to 9 October 2022, adults who paid their gas or electricity by prepayment (72%) more frequently reported difficulty affording energy than those who pay for gas and electricity using either direct debit or one-off payments (42%).

2. Latest experiences of increasing cost of living, difficulty or being behind with energy, rent or mortgage payments

Cost of living increases

According to our latest Public opinions and social trends, Great Britain: 29 September to 9 October 2022 bulletin (https://www.ons.gov.uk/peoplepopulationandcommunity/wellbeing/bulletins/publicopinionsandsocialtrendsgreatbritain/29septemberto9october2022), around 9 in 10 (93%) reported their cost of living had increased compared with a year ago. A lower percentage (79%) reported an increase in their cost of living over the last month.

Increases in the cost of living are affecting different adults in different ways. For example, when looking at the experiences of adults who pay their energy bills (gas or electricity) by prepayment, around 7 in 10 (72%) reported difficulty in affording their energy, compared with 4 in 10 (42%) who paid for their gas and electricity by either direct debit or one-off payments when they received a bill (Figure 1).

Figure 1: Around 7 in 10 (72%) who paid by prepayment ("top up") for their energy reported difficulty affording it

Proportion reporting difficulty (very or somewhat) affording energy payments among adults responsible, by method of payment, Great Britain, 28 September to 9 October 2022

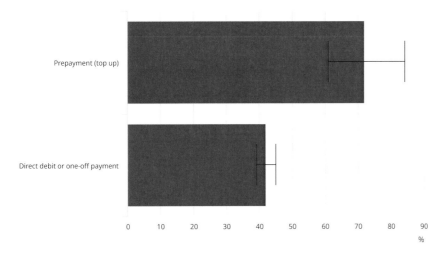

Source: Office for National Statistics (ONS) – Opinions and Lifestyle Survey (OPN)

Notes:

1. Questions: "How easy or difficult is it to afford your energy bills?" and "How does your household pay for gas or electricity?".

2. Base: Adults who pay energy bills.

3. Respondents were included in the prepayment ("top up") group if they paid for either gas or electricity using a top up meter via a key, card or app.

This finding is reflected in the latest data from Citizens Advice (https://public.flourish.studio/story/1634399/), which shows that the number of people seeking their advice who say that they cannot afford to top up their prepayment meter, has increased rapidly in the past year. These data also shows that across different groups of the population who seek their advice, people are more likely to request support with cost of living issues than ever before.

3. Characteristics of adults who are experiencing difficulty or are behind with energy, rent or mortgage payments

The estimates shown in this section are based on the period 22 June to 11 September 2022 ("latest pooled period"), providing us with a larger pool of data to examine the experiences of different groups of the population.

Estimates are also provided for the earlier period of 30 March to 19 June 2022 ("previous pooled period") and 6 January to 27 February 2022, where available.

These data were collected during a year in which the energy price cap (https://www.ofgem.gov.uk/information-consumers/energy-advice-households/check-if-energy-price-cap-affects-you) increased from the start of April 2022 and then further from the start of October 2022, with a government package of support for energy bills (https://www.gov.uk/government/publications/energy-bills-support/energy-bills-support-factsheet-8-september-2022) taking effect from 1 October 2022.

In 2021 in the UK, people's mortgage payments represented on average around 16% of their income, as shown in our House Price Index: annual tables 20 to 39 dataset (https://www.ons.gov.uk/economy/inflationandpriceindices/datasets/housepriceindexannualtables2039). In England in 2020, renters on the average income could expect to spend around a quarter (23%) of their income on an average priced home, as shown in our Private rental affordability, England: 2012 to 2020 bulletin (https://www.ons.gov.uk/peoplepopulationandcommunity/housing/bulletins/privaterentalaffordabilityengland/latest).

People's rent or mortgage costs are also increasing. According to the latest experimental data from our Index of Private Housing Rental Prices, UK bulletin (https://www.ons.gov.uk/economy/inflationandpriceindices/bulletins/indexofprivatehousingrentalprices/september2022), private rental prices paid by tenants in the UK rose by 3.6% in the 12 months to September 2022, up from 3.4% in the 12 months to August 2022. These data were collected prior to the recent volatility in the mortgage market.

All adults

The proportion reporting finding it difficult to afford their energy bills, rent or mortgage payments has increased through the year.

- In the latest pooled period, almost half of adults (45%) who paid energy bills reported it being difficult (very or somewhat) to afford them (40% in the previous pooled period)

- Of adults who were paying rent or had mortgage payments, 3 in 10 (30%) reported finding it difficult to afford these payments (26% in the previous pooled period, Figure 2).

Figure 2: The proportion of people finding it difficult to afford their energy, rent or mortgage payments is increasing

Proportions reporting difficulty (very or somewhat) affording energy, rent or mortgage payments, among adults responsible for them, all adults, Great Britain, March to June 2022 and June to September 2022

Source: Office for National Statistics - Opinions and Lifestyle Survey (OPN)

Notes:

1. Questions: "How easy or difficult is it to afford your energy bills?" and "How easy or difficult is it to afford your rent or mortgage payments?".

2. Base: Adults who pay energy bills or adults who are making rent or mortgage payments.

3. The indicated questions and bases also apply to Figures 3, 5, 7, 10, 12 and 14.

4. Figures 2 to 13 shown in this release are based on unrounded data to allow for the clearest indication of the 95% confidence intervals around the estimates provided. Data are available rounded to the nearest whole number in the chart download files and the associated dataset.

Download the data

.xlsx (https://www.ons.gov.uk/visualisations/dvc2198/2-all-adults-difficulty/datadownload.xlsx)

The proportion of adults who reported being behind on these bills was relatively similar across the two pooled periods. In the latest pooled period, 3% of adults reported being behind on their rent or mortgage payments, and 5% reported being behind on their energy bills (2% and 4% in the previous pooled period, respectively).

Disability status

Disabled (https://analysisfunction.civilservice.gov.uk/policy-store/measuring-disability-for-the-equality-act-2010/) adults were more likely than non-disabled adults to find it difficult to afford their energy bills, rent or mortgage payments. They were also more likely to report being behind.

Over half (55%) of disabled adults reported finding it difficult to afford their energy bills, and around a third (36%) found it difficult to afford their rent or mortgage payments compared with 40% and 27% of non-disabled people, respectively, in the latest pooled period.

Around 1 in 15 (7%) disabled adults reported being behind on their energy bills compared with around 1 in 25 (4%) non-disabled people. Around 1 in 25 (4%) disabled adults reported being behind on their rent or mortgage payments compared with 1 in 50 (2%) non-disabled people (Figure 3 and Figure 4).

Figure 3: Disabled adults were more likely than non-disabled adults to find it difficult to afford their energy, rent or mortgage payments

Proportions reporting difficulty (very or somewhat) affording energy, rent or mortgage payments, among adults responsible for them, by disability status, Great Britain, March to June 2022 and June to September 2022

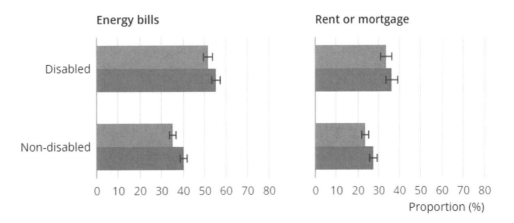

Source: Office for National Statistics - Opinions and Lifestyle Survey (OPN)

Notes:

1. Questions: "How easy or difficult is it to afford your energy bills?" and "How easy or difficult is it to afford your rent or mortgage payments?".

2. Base: Adults who pay energy bills or adults who are making rent or mortgage payments.

Download the data

.xlsx (https://www.ons.gov.uk/visualisations/dvc2198/3-disability-difficulty/datadownload.xlsx)

Figure 4: Disabled adults were more likely than non-disabled adults to be behind with their energy, rent or mortgage payments

Proportions reporting being behind on energy, rent or mortgage payments, among adults who have gas or electricity supplied to their home or who make rent or mortgage payments, by disability status, Great Britain, March to June 2022 and June to September 2022

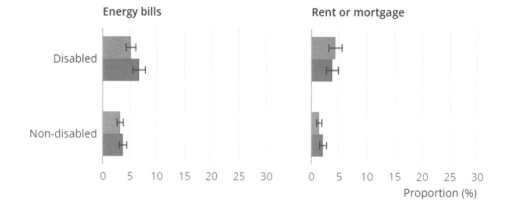

Source: Office for National Statistics - Opinions and Lifestyle Survey (OPN)

Notes:

1. Questions: "Are you behind on payments for your gas or electricity bills?" and "Are you behind on your rent or mortgage payments?".

2. Base: Adults who said they have gas or electricity supplied to their home or adults who are currently paying rent or mortgage.

3. The indicated questions and bases also apply to Figures 6, 8, 11 and 13.

Download the data

.xlsx (https://www.ons.gov.uk/visualisations/dvc2198/4-disability-behind/datadownload.xlsx)

Ethnicity

Around 4 in 10 (44%) White adults reported finding it difficult to afford their energy bills. This proportion appeared to be highest among Black or Black British adults (69%) and Asian or Asian British adults (59%).

Around a quarter (28%) of White adults reported finding it difficult to afford their rent or mortgage payments. This proportion also appeared highest among Black or Black British adults (52%) (Figure 5).

Around 1 in 25 (4%) White adults reported being behind on their energy bills. This proportion appeared highest among Black or Black British adults (21%).

Around 1 in 50 (2%) White adults reported being behind on their rent or mortgage payments. This proportion appeared highest among Black or Black British (9%), Mixed or Multiple ethnic group (9%) and Asian or Asian British (8%) adults (Figure 6).

Estimates by ethnic group (for example Black or Black British) provided in this section and the accompanying dataset (https://www.ons.gov.uk/peoplepopulationandcommunity/personalandhouseholdfinances/expenditure/datasets/impactofincreasedcostoflivingonadultsacrossgreatbritain) are based on relatively small sample sizes, and so should be treated with caution. Differences between some ethnic groups were not statistically significant, and therefore confidence intervals (https://www.ons.gov.uk/methodology/methodologytopicsandstatisticalconcepts/uncertaintyandhowwemeasureit#confidence-interval) should be used to assess the statistical significance (https://www.ons.gov.uk/methodology/methodologytopicsandstatisticalconcepts/uncertaintyandhowwemeasureit#statistical-significance) of any differences.

Figure 5: Black or Black British adults and Asian or Asian British adults appeared more likely than White adults to find it difficult to afford their energy bills, rent or mortgage payments

Proportions reporting difficulty (very or somewhat) affording energy, rent or mortgage payments, among adults responsible for them, by ethnicity, Great Britain, June to September 2022

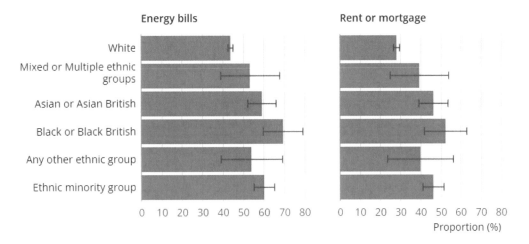

Source: Office for National Statistics - Opinions and Lifestyle Survey (OPN)

Download the data

.xlsx (https://www.ons.gov.uk/visualisations/dvc2198/5-ethnicity-difficulty/datadownload.xlsx)

Figure 6: Black or Black British, Mixed or Multiple ethnicity and Asian or Asian British adults appeared more likely than White adults to be behind on their energy bills, rent or mortgage payments

Proportions among adults who have gas or electricity supplied to their home or make rent or mortgage payments by ethnicity, Great Britain, June to September 2022

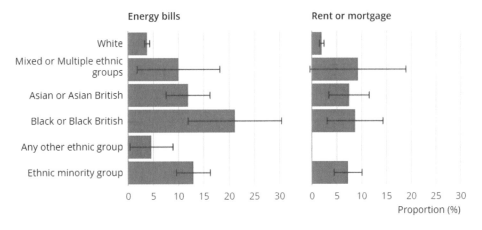

Source: Office for National Statistics - Opinions and Lifestyle Survey (OPN)

Notes:

1. Estimates of the proportion behind on rent or mortgage payments are not provided for the category "Any other ethnic group" due to small sample size.

Download the data

.xlsx (https://www.ons.gov.uk/visualisations/dvc2198/6-ethnicity-behind/datadownload.xlsx)

Renters

Adults who were renting their home were more likely than those currently paying a mortgage to find it difficult to afford or be behind with their energy bills, rent or mortgage payments.

Around 6 in 10 (60%) renters reported finding it difficult to afford their energy bills compared with around 4 in 10 (43%) of those with a mortgage in the latest pooled period. Around a third (35%) of those who owned their home outright reported finding it difficult to afford their energy bills.

Around 4 in 10 (39%) renters found it difficult to afford their rent payments compared with 23% of mortgagors who found it difficult to pay their mortgage.

Around 1 in 10 (11%) renters reported being behind on their energy bills compared with 3% of those with a mortgage and 1% among those who owned their home outright. Around 1 in 20 (5%) renters reported being behind on their rent payments compared with 1 in 100 (1%) of those with a mortgage (Figure 7 and Figure 8).

The difference in the responses of renters and mortgagors here likely reflects some mortgagors being on fixed rate mortgages, whereas renters may be more exposed to increases in rent. According to the latest experimental data from our Index of Private Housing Rental Prices, UK bulletin (https://www.ons.gov.uk/economy/inflationandpriceindices/bulletins/indexofprivatehousingrentalprices/september2022), private rental prices paid by tenants in the UK rose by 3.6% in the 12 months to September 2022, up from 3.4% in the 12 months to August 2022.

Figure 7: Adults who were renting their home were more likely than those paying a mortgage to find it difficult to afford their energy, rent or mortgage payments

Proportions reporting difficulty (very or somewhat) affording energy, rent or mortgage payments, among adults responsible for them, by tenure, Great Britain, March to June 2022 and June to September 2022

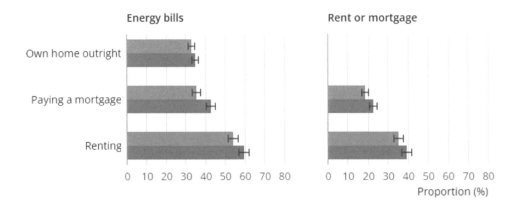

Source: Office for National Statistics - Opinions and Lifestyle Survey (OPN)

Notes:

1. Estimates are not shown for difficult to afford rent or mortgages among the category "Own home outright".

Download the data

.xlsx (https://www.ons.gov.uk/visualisations/dvc2198/7-tenure-difficulty/datadownload.xlsx)

Figure 8: Adults who were renting their home were more likely than those paying a mortgage to be behind on their energy, rent or mortgage payments

Proportions reporting being behind on energy, rent or mortgage payments, among adults who have gas or electricity supplied to their home or who make rent or mortgage payments, by tenure, Great Britain, March to June 2022 and June to September 2022

Source: Office for National Statistics - Opinions and Lifestyle Survey (OPN)

Notes:

1. The estimates of being behind on mortgage or rent payments for the category "Paying a mortgage" is not shown for March to June 2022 because of being less than 1%. Estimates of being behind on mortgage or rent payments are not shown for the category "Own home outright".

Download the data

.xlsx (https://www.ons.gov.uk/visualisations/dvc2198/8-tenure-behind/datadownload.xlsx)

Younger and older people

Younger adults (aged 16 to 24 years) were less likely to report a general increase in their cost of living during the past month in the latest pooled period, possibly because some people in this population are not yet bill payers.

Following a trend seen across all age groups, the proportion of those aged 16 to 24 years reporting an increase in their cost of living has risen from 42%, in the pooled period 6 January to 27 February 2022, to 78% in the most recent pooled period (Figure 9).

Figure 9: Younger adults are gradually becoming more likely to report an increase in their general cost of living in the past month compared with earlier in 2022

Proportion of adults reporting an increase in their cost of living over the last month, by age group, Great Britain, 6 January to 27 February 2022, 30 March to 19 June 2022 and 22 June to 11 September 2022

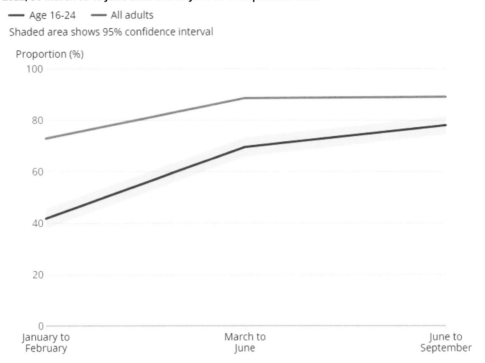

Source: Office for National Statistics - Opinions and Lifestyle Survey (OPN)

Notes:

1. Question: "Over the last month, has your cost of living changed?".

2. Base: All adults.

Download the data

.xlsx (https://www.ons.gov.uk/visualisations/dvc2198/9-age-costofliving/datadownload.xlsx)

Adults in the youngest and oldest age groups appeared less likely to report having difficulty with or being behind on rent or mortgage payments. This possibly reflects younger people not yet being responsible for such payments and older people being more likely to own their home outright.

Around a quarter of younger or older adults reported difficulty affording rent or mortgage payments. By age group, this was:

- 22% of adults aged 16 to 24 years

- 28% of adults aged 65 to 74 years

- 26% of adults aged 75 years and over

This is compared with around a third in other age groups, which was:

- 31% of adults aged 25 to 34 years

- 34% of adults aged 35 to 44 years

- 30% of adults aged 45 to 54 years

- 34% of adults aged 55 to 64 years

For more information, see Figure 10 and Figure 11.

Figure 10: Adults in younger or older age groups appeared less likely than in other age groups to find it difficult to afford their energy bills, rent or mortgage payments

Proportions reporting difficulty (very or somewhat) affording energy, rent or mortgage payments, among adults responsible for them, by age group, Great Britain, June to September 2022

Source: Office for National Statistics - Opinions and Lifestyle Survey (OPN)

Download the data

.xlsx (https://www.ons.gov.uk/visualisations/dvc2198/10-age-difficulty/datadownload.xlsx)

Figure 11: Adults in younger or older age groups appeared less likely than in other age groups to be behind on their energy bills, rent or mortgage payments

Proportions reporting being behind on energy, rent or mortgage payments, among adults who have gas or electricity supplied to their home or who make rent or mortgage payments, by age group, Great Britain, June to September 2022

Source: Office for National Statistics - Opinions and Lifestyle Survey (OPN)

Notes:

1. Estimates of being behind on rent or mortgage payments are not shown for the category "75 and older" due to being less than 1%.

Download the data

.xlsx (https://www.ons.gov.uk/visualisations/dvc2198/11-age-behind/datadownload.xlsx)

Region

A relatively similar proportion of adults across the different regions and countries of Great Britain reported finding it difficult to pay their energy bills (ranging from 40% to 51% by region).

However, adults in the North East (9%) and London (9%) appeared to be slightly more likely than in some other regions to be behind with their energy bills, with this proportion ranging from 2% to 9% depending on region.

Adults in London appeared to be the most likely to report finding it difficult to pay their rent or mortgage (37%).

Adults in the North West (5%) and London (5%) appeared to be more likely than in some other regions to be behind with their rent or mortgage payments, with this proportion ranging from 1% to 5% depending on region (Figure 12 and Figure 13).

It is likely that many of the differences between regions noted here may be linked to an association between region and other demographic characteristics. For example, the age profile of London is younger than the rest of Great Britain, with the average age of Londoners almost five years below the UK average in 2020. The average house price in London is also higher than in any other region in the UK. For more information on the average age of Londoners, see our Population estimates for the UK, England and Wales, Scotland and Northern Ireland: mid-2020 bulletin. (https://www.ons.gov.uk/peoplepopulationandcommunity/populationandmigration/populationestimates/bulletins/annualmidyearpopulatio nestimates/mid2020) For more information on the average house price in London, see our UK House Price Index: August 2022 bulletin (https://www.ons.gov.uk/economy/inflationandpriceindices/bulletins/housepriceindex/august2022).

Figure 12: Adults in London appeared more likely than in other regions to find it difficult to afford their rent or mortgage payments

Proportions reporting difficulty (very or somewhat) affording energy, rent or mortgage payments, among adults responsible for them, by region and country, Great Britain, June to September 2022

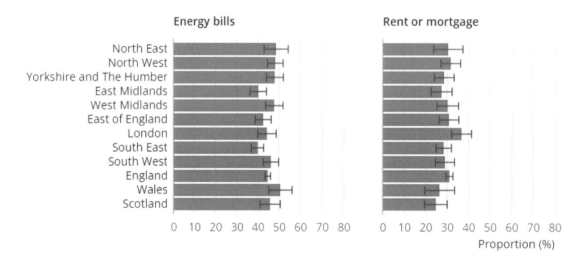

Source: Office for National Statistics - Opinions and Lifestyle Survey (OPN)

Download the data

.xlsx (https://www.ons.gov.uk/visualisations/dvc2198/12-region-difficulty/datadownload.xlsx)

Figure 13: Adults in the North East and London appeared to be more likely than in other regions to be behind on their energy bills

Proportions reporting being behind on energy, rent or mortgage payments, among adults who have gas or electricity supplied to their home or who make rent or mortgage payments, by region and country, Great Britain, June to September 2022

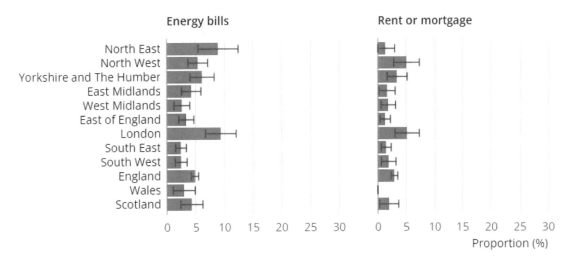

Source: Office for National Statistics - Opinions and Lifestyle Survey (OPN)

Notes:

1. Estimates of being behind on rent or mortgage payments are not shown for the category "Wales" due to small sample size.

Download the data

.xlsx (https://www.ons.gov.uk/visualisations/dvc2198/13-region-behind/datadownload.xlsx)

Economic factors

Economic factors, such as personal income, employment status or level of deprivation of the area they live in (based on the Index of Multiple Deprivation (https://www.gov.uk/government/collections/english-indices-of-deprivation)), also appeared to affect peoples' experiences of difficulty or being behind on energy, rent or mortgage payments.

For example, those on lower incomes more frequently reported finding it difficult to afford their energy bills in the current pooled period.

Around half of those with a personal income of less than £20,000 per year said they found it difficult to afford their energy bills. This proportion decreased as personal income increased, with around a quarter (23%) of those earning £50,000 or more reporting this (Figure 14).

A similar trend can be seen in difficulty affording rent or mortgage payments, with those with higher personal incomes finding it less difficult to afford such payments.

Figure 14: Adults with lower personal income were more likely to find it difficult to afford their energy, rent or mortgage payments

Proportions reporting difficulty (very or somewhat) affording energy, rent or mortgage payments, among adults responsible for them, by region and country, Great Britain, June to September 2022

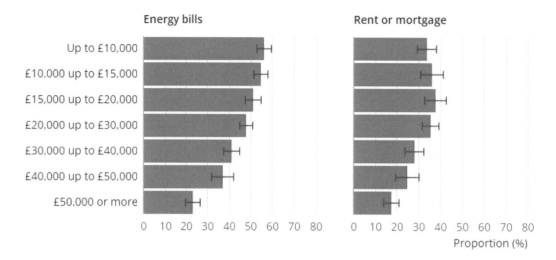

Source: Office for National Statistics - Opinions and Lifestyle Survey (OPN)

Download the data

.xlsx (https://www.ons.gov.uk/visualisations/dvc2198/14-income-difficulty/datadownload.xlsx)

In the current pooled period, the proportions reporting being behind on energy, rent or mortgage payments appeared to follow this trend. For example, ranging from 6% reporting being behind on their energy payments among those on lower incomes (between £10,000 and £15,000, and between £15,000 and £20,000) to 2% among those earning more than £50,000.

The accompanying dataset (https://www.ons.gov.uk/peoplepopulationandcommunity/personalandhouseholdfinances/expenditure/datasets/impactofincreasedcostoflivingonadultsacrossgreatbritain) contains estimates for all other breakdowns analysed but not discussed in this article. They include estimates by:

- employment status
- level of deprivation of the area a person lives in
- highest education level
- parental status
- marital status
- housing size

The reasons why the proportion of people reporting having difficulty or being behind with their energy, rent or mortgage payments varies by individual characteristics are likely complex, as there are often associations between the individual characteristics considered.

For a regression analysis considering which adults have been most likely to be impacted by increased cost of living after controlling for a range of personal characteristics, please see our Impact of increased cost of living on adults across Great Britain: November 2021 to March 2022 article (https://www.ons.gov.uk/peoplepopulationandcommunity/personalandhouseholdfinances/expenditure/articles/impactofincreasedcostoflivingonadultsacrossgreatbritain/november2021tomarch2022#characteristics-of-adults-who-are-unable-to-afford-an-unexpected-expense).

4. Impact of increased cost of living on adults across Great Britain data

Impact of increased cost of living on adults across Great Britain
(https://www.ons.gov.uk/peoplepopulationandcommunity/personalandhouseholdfinances/expenditure/datasets/impactofincreasedcost
oflivingonadultsacrossgreatbritain)

Dataset | Released 25 October 2022

People in Great Britain's experiences of and actions following increases in their costs of living, and how these differed by a range of
personal characteristics.

5. Glossary

Disability status

To define disability in this publication, we refer to the Government Statistical Service (GSS) harmonised "core" definition of disability (https://analysisfunction.civilservice.gov.uk/policy-store/measuring-disability-for-the-equality-act-2010/): this identifies "disabled" as a person who has a physical or mental health condition or illness that has lasted or is expected to last 12 months or more that reduces their ability to carry-out day-to-day activities. The GSS harmonised questions are asked of the respondent in the survey, meaning that disability status is self-reported.

Ethnicity

The ethnicity disaggregation used has been chosen to provide the most granular breakdown possible, while producing robust estimates based on sample sizes, in line with the GSS ethnicity harmonised standard (https://analysisfunction.civilservice.gov.uk/policy-store/ethnicity-harmonised-standard/).

The five-category ethnicity breakdown includes:

- White: White British, White Irish, Other White
- Mixed and Multiple ethnic groups: White and Black Caribbean, White and Black African, White and Asian or Any other Mixed and Multiple ethnic background
- Asian or Asian British: Indian, Pakistani, Bangladeshi, Chinese or any other Asian background
- Black or Black British: African, Caribbean or Any other Black, African or Caribbean background
- Other ethnic background group: Arab or Any other ethnic group

Statistical significance

This article presents a summary of results, with further data including confidence intervals (https://www.ons.gov.uk/methodology/methodologytopicsandstatisticalconcepts/uncertaintyandhowwemeasureit#confidence-interval) for the estimates shown in the charts presented and contained in the associated datasets. Where comparisons between groups are presented, 95% confidence intervals should be used to assess the statistical significance (https://www.ons.gov.uk/methodology/methodologytopicsandstatisticalconcepts/uncertaintyandhowwemeasureit#statistical-significance) of the change.

Other definitions

A definition of all breakdowns of estimates used within this article are available in more detail within the Notes tab of the accompanying dataset (https://www.ons.gov.uk/peoplepopulationandcommunity/personalandhouseholdfinances/expenditure/datasets/impactofincreasedcostoflivingonadultsacrossgreatbritain).

6. Data sources and quality

This release contains data and indicators from the Office for National Statistics' (ONS) Opinions and Lifestyle Survey.

Quality

More quality and methodology information on the Opinions and Lifestyle Survey (OPN) and its strengths, limitations, appropriate uses, and how the data were created is available in our Opinions and Lifestyle Survey Quality and Methodology Information (https://www.ons.gov.uk/peoplepopulationandcommunity/healthandsocialcare/healthandlifeexpectancies/methodologies/opinionsandlifestylesurveyqmi).

Sampling

The analysis throughout this article is based on adults aged 16 years and over in Great Britain. The latest analysis in this report is based on 13,305 adults from a pooled dataset comprising six waves of data collection, covering the following periods:

- 22 June to 3 July 2022
- 6 to 17 July 2022
- 20 to 31 July 2022
- 3 to 14 August 2022
- 17 to 29 August 2022
- 31 August to 11 September 2022

Pooling six waves of data together increases sample sizes, and allows us to carry out detailed analysis for different groups of the population.

Weighting

Survey weights were applied to make estimates representative of the population.

Weights were adjusted for non-response. Subsequently, the weights were calibrated considering the following factors: sex by age, region, tenure, education and employment status.

For age, sex and region, population totals based on projections of mid-year population estimates for June 2021 were used. The resulting weighted sample is therefore representative of the Great Britain adult population by a number of socio-demographic factors and geography.

7. Related links

The cost of living, current and upcoming work: September 2022

(https://www.ons.gov.uk/economy/inflationandpriceindices/articles/thecostoflivingcurrentandupcomingwork/september2022)

Article | Released 28 September 2022

A summary of ONS' current and future analytical work related to the cost of living.

Parents more likely to report increases in their cost of living

(https://www.ons.gov.uk/peoplepopulationandcommunity/personalandhouseholdfinances/expenditure/articles/parentsmorelikelytoreportincreasesintheircostofliving/2022-09-07)

Article | Released 7 September 2022

Parents were more likely to report using credit more than usual because of rising costs in spring 2022. With prices for essentials such as food and energy rising, how does household composition affect finances?

What actions are people taking because of the rising cost of living?

(http://www.ons.gov.uk/releases/whatactionsarepeopletakingbecauseoftherisingcostoflivingmarchtojune2022)

Article | Released 5 August 2022

Estimates from the Opinions and Lifestyle Survey (OPN) regarding increases in cost of living and the actions adults in Great Britain are taking as a result, by breakdowns including disability status, personal income, area deprivation and region, for the period 30 March to 19 June 2022.

Impact of increased cost of living on adults across Great Britain: November 2021 to March 2022

(https://www.ons.gov.uk/peoplepopulationandcommunity/personalandhouseholdfinances/expenditure/articles/impactofincreasedcostoflivingonadultsacrossgreatbritain/november2021tomarch2022)

Article | Released 30 March 2022

Analysis of the proportion of the population affected by an increase in their cost of living and the individual characteristics associated with not being able to afford an unexpected expense, using data from the Opinions and Lifestyle Survey (OPN).

The rising cost of living and its impact on individuals in Great Britain: November 2021 to March 2022

(https://www.ons.gov.uk/peoplepopulationandcommunity/personalandhouseholdfinances/expenditure/articles/therisingcostoflivinganditsimpactonindividualsingreatbritain/november2021tomarch2022)

Article | Released 25 April 2022

Analysis of how different groups in the population have been affected by an increase in their cost of living, using data from the Opinions and Lifestyle Survey (OPN).

Public opinions and social trends, Great Britain

(https://www.ons.gov.uk/peoplepopulationandcommunity/wellbeing/bulletins/publicopinionsandsocialtrendsgreatbritain/29septembert o9october2022)

Statistical bulletin | Released on 14 October 2022

Social insights on daily life and events, including the cost of living, location of work, health and well-being from the Opinions and Lifestyle Survey (OPN).

Economic activity and social change in the UK, real-time indicators

(https://www.ons.gov.uk/economy/economicoutputandproductivity/output/bulletins/economicactivityandsocialchangeintheukrealtimein dicators/latest)

Statistical bulletin | Released weekly

Early experimental data and analysis on economic activity and social change in the UK. These real-time indicators are created using rapid response surveys, novel data sources and experimental methods.

Energy efficiency of housing in England and Wales: 2022
(https://www.ons.gov.uk/releases/energyefficiencyofhousinginenglandandwales2022)

Statistical bulletin | Released on 25 October 2022

Insight on the energy efficiency, environmental impact, carbon dioxide emissions and central heating main fuel type for new and existing homes by property type, tenure and property age.

Tracking the price of the lowest-cost grocery items, UK, experimental analysis: April 2021 to September 2022
(https://www.ons.gov.uk/releases/trackingthepriceofthelowestcostgroceryitemsukexperimentalanalysisapril2021toseptember2022)

Statistical bulletin | Released on 25 October 2022

How the prices of the lowest-cost products for 30 everyday items have changed since April 2021.

8. Cite this statistical article

Office for National Statistics (ONS), released 25 October 2022, ONS website, article, Impact of increased cost of living on adults across Great Britain: June to September 2022
(https://www.ons.gov.uk/releases/impactofincreasedcostoflivingonadultsacrossgreatbritainjunetoseptember2022)

Contact details for this article

Caleb Ogwuru, Laura Fairey, David Ainslie and Tim Vizard
policy.evidence.analysis@ons.gov.uk
Telephone: +44 300 0671543

You might also be interested in:

Cost of living latest insights tool

Office for
National Statistics

Data and analysis from Census 2021

Impact of increased cost of living on adults across Great Britain: September 2022 to January 2023

Analysis of the proportion of the population that are affected by an increase in their cost of living, and of the characteristics associated with financial vulnerability, using data from the Opinions and Lifestyle survey.

Contact:
Jodie Davis, Unity Amoaku, Simeon North, Henry Beevor and Tim Vizard

Release date:
20 February 2023

Next release:
To be announced

Table of contents

1. Main points

In this article, we have identified groups experiencing some form of financial vulnerability. In the latest pooled period, 14 September 2022 to 8 January 2023, we found:

- renters had higher odds of experiencing some form of financial vulnerability (4.4 higher odds), compared with those who own their home outright; more than half (55%) of renters reported being unable to afford an unexpected, but necessary, expense of £850, compared with 12% of outright homeowners

- adults aged 25 to 34 years had the highest odds of experiencing some form of financial vulnerability (2.2 higher odds), compared with those aged 75 years and over; around a third of adults aged 25 to 34 years (34%) reported borrowing more money or using more credit than usual compared with a year ago, compared with 7% of those aged 75 years and over

- parents living with dependent children aged 0 to 4 years and aged 5 years and over had higher odds of experiencing some form of financial vulnerability (3.5 and 4.1 higher odds respectively), compared with non-parents or parents not living with dependent children; around half (54%) of parents living with a dependent child reported being unable to save in the next 12 months, compared with 4 in 10 (42%) non-parents, or parents not living with a dependent child

- adults with a personal annual income of £10,000 up to £15,000 had the highest odds of experiencing some form of financial vulnerability (4.3 higher odds), compared with adults earning £50,000 or more per year; a higher proportion of adults earning £10,000 up to £15,000 per year reported being unable to save in the next 12 months (56%), compared with 24% of those earning £50,000 or more per year

- adults who pay for their gas or electricity through prepayment meters were almost twice as likely to report using credit more than usual, through things such as credit cards and loans, because of the increases in the cost of living (26%), than those who do not pay for their gas and electricity through a prepayment method (14%)

2. Experiences of increased cost of living

Cost of living increases and actions taken

Our Public opinions and social trends, Great Britain bulletin
(https://www.ons.gov.uk/peoplepopulationandcommunity/wellbeing/bulletins/publicopinionsandsocialtrendsgreatbritain/25januaryto5february2023) found that during the latest survey period, 25 January to 5 February 2023, over 9 in 10 (94%) adults reported their cost of living had increased compared with a year ago. A lower proportion (69%) reported an increase over the last month.

The most commonly reported reasons given by adults for the rise in their cost of living during this period were related to increases in the price of their food shop (95%), their gas or electricity bills (73%) and the price of their fuel (39%).

When asked what they were doing because of increases in the cost of living, around 7 in 10 (69%) adults said they were spending less on non-essentials, while 60% said they were using less fuel, such as gas or electricity in their home. These were the most commonly reported actions by all adults across Great Britain.

Throughout the rest of this article, we have used a larger pooled dataset covering 14 September 2022 to 8 January 2023 (the "latest pooled period"), to explore how the rising cost of living is impacting different groups of the population. This article highlights some of these differences, however further data can be found in the accompanying dataset.
(https://www.ons.gov.uk/peoplepopulationandcommunity/personalandhouseholdfinances/expenditure/datasets/impactofincreasedcostoflivingonadultsacrossgreatbritain)

Using less fuel, such as gas or electricity in home

In April 2022, the energy price cap (https://www.ofgem.gov.uk/information-consumers/energy-advice-households/check-if-energy-price-cap-affects-you) was increased, meaning households were paying more for their energy use. The government's Energy Bills Support Scheme (https://www.gov.uk/get-help-energy-bills/getting-discount-energy-bill) and the Energy Price Guarantee (https://www.gov.uk/government/publications/energy-bills-support/energy-bills-support-factsheet-8-september-2022) came into effect in October 2022, that may have affected the behaviours of individuals in this pooled dataset.

In addition to government support to limit household expenditure on energy bills, some groups were more likely to say they were using less gas or electricity in their home because of the increased cost of living, with 62% of all adults selecting this in the latest pooled period.

Similar to findings reported in our article looking at the actions people are taking because of the rising cost of living (https://www.ons.gov.uk/peoplepopulationandcommunity/personalandhouseholdfinances/expenditure/articles/whatactionsarepeopletakingbecauseoftherisingcostofliving/latest), we found those more likely to report using less gas or electricity in their home included:

- around 7 in 10 adults aged 55 to 64 years (72%) and 65 to 74 years (70%), compared with 40% of those aged 16 to 24 years
- homeowners and those paying off a mortgage (66% and 64% respectively), compared with 55% of renters
- two-thirds (66%) of parents living with dependent children aged 5 years and over, compared with 61% of non-parents or parents not living with dependent children
- two-thirds (66%) of adults who do not pay for their gas or electricity through a prepayment meter, compared with 54% of those who pay for their energy through such means.

Figure 1: Adults aged 55 to 74 years were among the most likely to report using less fuel in their home because of the increased cost of living

Proportions of adults reporting using less fuel such as gas or electricity in their home because of increases in the cost of living, by a range of characteristics, September 2022 to January 2023

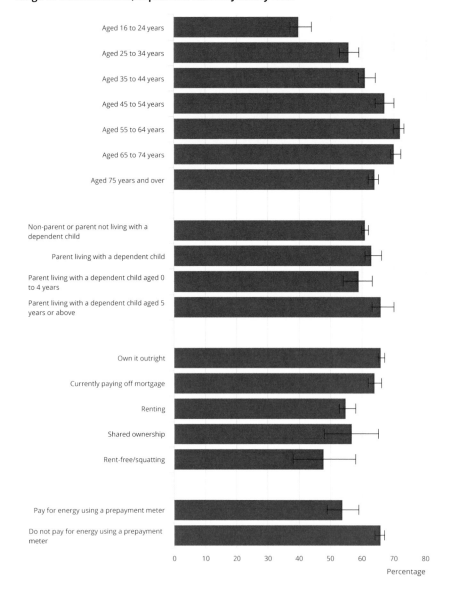

Source: Office for National Statistics – Opinions and Lifestyle Survey (OPN)

Notes:

1. Parent living with a dependent child has been split into two further groups: parent living with a dependent child aged 0 to 4 years and parent living with a dependent child aged 5 years and over.

Using credit more than usual

With the cost of living rising, 15% of adults reported borrowing more than usual by using credit cards, their overdraft, or taking out a loan. While loans can provide short-term financial security, the increased use of credit can pose longer-term challenges for households.

Adults aged 25 to 34 years and 35 to 44 years were more likely to report having to use credit more than usual (26% and 23%, respectively) because of the increased cost of living, compared with both their younger and older counterparts.

A higher proportion of adults living in the most deprived areas of England also reported having to use credit more than usual (19%), compared with those in the least deprived areas (11%). Renters were four times more likely to report this action (22%), compared with adults who own their home outright (5%).

Parents living with dependent children were more likely to report using credit more than usual because of the rising cost of living (27%), compared with non-parents or parents not living with dependent children (12%). This higher rate appears to be driven by parents living with younger children (aged 0 to 4 years), with 30% selecting this action.

Adults who pay for their gas or electricity through prepayment meters were almost twice as likely to report using credit more than usual (26%) than those who do not pay for their gas and electricity through a prepayment method (14%).

Figure 2: Parents living with dependent children were among the most likely to report using credit more than usual because of the increased cost of living

Proportions of adults reporting using credit more than usual because of increases in the cost of living, by a range of characteristics, September 2022 to January 2023

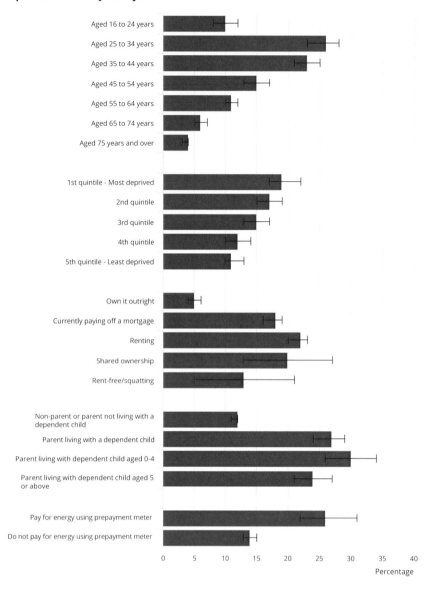

Source: Office for National Statistics – Opinions and Lifestyle Survey (OPN)

Notes:

1. Area deprivation covers England only. For more information, see Section 5: Glossary. (https://www.ons.gov.uk/peoplepopulationandcommunity/personalandhouseholdfinances/expenditure/articles/impactofincreasedcosto flivingonadultsacrossgreatbritain/september2022tojanuary2023#glossary)

2. Parent living with a dependent child has been split into two further groups: parent living with a dependent child aged 0 to 4 years and parent living with a dependent child aged 5 years and over.

3. Characteristics associated with financial vulnerability

In our March 2022 article
(https://www.ons.gov.uk/peoplepopulationandcommunity/personalandhouseholdfinances/expenditure/articles/impactofincreasedcostofliving
onadultsacrossgreatbritain/november2021tomarch2022), we explored the characteristics associated with not being able to afford an
unexpected, but necessary, expense of £850. In this article, we have expanded our measure of financial vulnerability to include three
additional questions.

In the latest pooled period, we found that around a quarter (23%) of adults experienced some form of financial vulnerability. In this article, a
person is considered to have experienced some form of financial vulnerability if three or more of the following applied to them:

- being unable to afford an unexpected, but necessary, expense of £850

- borrowing more money or using more credit than usual, in the last month, compared to a year ago

- being unable to save in the next 12 months

- finding it very or somewhat difficult to afford energy bills

This section presents findings from a logistic regression, that assesses the likelihood of having some form of financial vulnerability, after
controlling for the following characteristics:

- age group

- sex

- region (including Wales and Scotland)

- disability status

- ethnicity

- employment status

- personal annual income

- highest education level

- housing tenure

- parental status

- household composition

After controlling for these characteristics, we found all factors to be associated with financial vulnerability, although no significant association
was found for ethnicity. This section explores some of these findings in more detail, with further data available in the accompanying dataset.
(https://www.ons.gov.uk/peoplepopulationandcommunity/personalandhouseholdfinances/expenditure/datasets/impactofincreasedcostofliving
ongonadultsacrossgreatbritain)

For more information on the regression analysis, please see Section 6: Data sources and quality.
(https://www.ons.gov.uk/peoplepopulationandcommunity/personalandhouseholdfinances/expenditure/articles/impactofincreasedcostofliving
gonadultsacrossgreatbritain/september2022tojanuary2023#data-sources-and-quality)

Age group

After controlling for a range of characteristics, adults aged 25 years and over were more likely to experience some form of financial
vulnerability when compared with those aged 75 years and over. Adults aged 25 to 34 years had the highest odds (odds ratio equals 2.2),
followed by those aged 45 to 54 years and 35 to 44 years (odds ratio equals 1.9).

A significant association was not found for those aged 16 to 24 years when compared with those aged 75 years and over. This may be explained by the fact that younger adults are more likely to live at home and therefore have less financial responsibilities. For more information, see our Young adults living with their parents dataset (https://www.ons.gov.uk/peoplepopulationandcommunity/birthsdeathsandmarriages/families/datasets/youngadultslivingwiththeirparents/current).

Figure 3: Adults aged 25 to 34 years had some of the highest odds among other age groups of experiencing some form of financial vulnerability, compared with those aged 75 years and over

Great Britain, September 2022 to January 2023

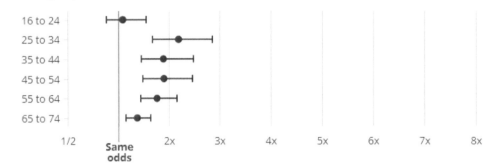

Source: Office for National Statistics (ONS) – Opinions and Lifestyle Survey (OPN)

Notes:

1. An odds ratio indicates the likelihood of experiencing some form of financial vulnerability given a particular characteristic.

Download the data

.xlsx (https://www.ons.gov.uk/visualisations/dvc2479/fig3/datadownload.xlsx)

When looking at the measures that contribute to financial vulnerability, we found that:

- a higher proportion of adults aged 25 to 34 years reported being unable to afford an unexpected, but necessary, expense of £850 (42%), when compared with those aged 75 years and over (16%)

- adults aged 25 to 34 years were also more likely to report borrowing more money or using more credit than usual compared to a year ago (34%), when compared with those aged 75 years and over (7%)

- adults aged 55 to 64 years were more likely to report being unable to save in the next 12 months (50%), compared with adults aged 16 to 24 years (32%) and 75 years and over (44%)

- adults aged 25 to 44 years who are responsible for paying energy bills were more likely to report finding it difficult to afford them (aged 25 to 34 years, 52%; aged 35 to 44 years, 52%), compared with all older age groups

Figure 4: Adults aged 25 to 34 years were more likely to report being unable to afford an unexpected expense of £850 and having to borrow more than usual compared with a year ago, compared with those aged 75 years and over

Proportion of people reporting the factors contributing to financial vulnerability by age group, Great Britain, September 2022 to January 2023

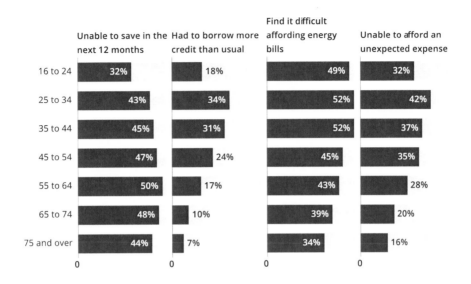

Source: Office for National Statistics (ONS) – Opinions and Lifestyle Survey (OPN)

Notes:

1. "Find it difficult affording energy bills" is among adults who were responsible for paying energy bills.

Download the data

.xlsx (https://www.ons.gov.uk/visualisations/dvc2479/fig4/datadownload.xlsx)

Personal annual income

After controlling for a range of characteristics, lower income groups were found to have some of the highest odds of experiencing some form of financial vulnerability. Adults with a personal income of £10,000 up to £15,000 per year had over four times higher odds of experiencing some form of financial vulnerability (odds ratio equals 4.3) than adults with an income of £50,000 or more per year. Adults in all other annual income groups below £50,000 were also significantly more likely to experience some form of financial vulnerability than adults with an income of £50,000 or more per year.

Figure 5: Adults on lower annual incomes had some of the highest odds of experiencing some form of financial vulnerability, compared with adults earning £50,000 or more per year

Great Britain, September 2022 to January 2023

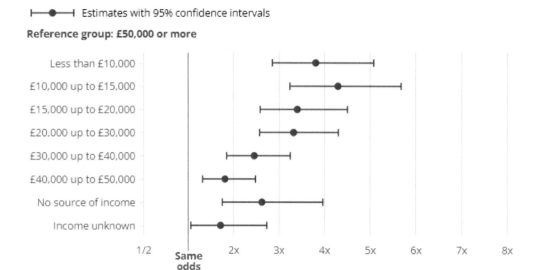

Source: Office for National Statistics (ONS) – Opinions and Lifestyle Survey (OPN)

Notes:

1. An odds ratio indicates the likelihood of being experiencing some form of financial vulnerability given a particular characteristic.

Download the data

.xlsx (https://www.ons.gov.uk/visualisations/dvc2479/fig5/datadownload.xlsx)

When looking at the measures that contribute to financial vulnerability, we found that:

- adults reporting a salary of up to £30,000 per year were more likely to report being unable to afford an unexpected expense of £850, compared with adults earning £30,000 or over

- a higher proportion of adults earning £20,000 to £30,000 per year reported borrowing more money or using more credit than usual compared with a year ago (26%), compared with those in the lowest income group (up to £10,000, 19%) and highest income group (£50,000 or more, 19%)

- adults reporting an annual salary of up to £15,000 were twice as likely to report being unable to save in the next 12 months (up to £10,000, 55%; £10,000 up to £15,000, 56%), compared with adults earning £50,000 or more per year (24%)

- adults responsible for paying energy bills in lower income groups were more likely to report finding it difficult to afford them, with 56% of those earning up to £10,000 per year reporting difficulty compared with 26% of those earning £50,000 or more

Figure 6: Adults earning £10,000 to £15,000 per year were more likely to report being unable to save in the next 12 months compared with the highest income group

Proportion of people reporting factors contributing to financial vulnerability by personal annual income, Great Britain, September 2022 to January 2023

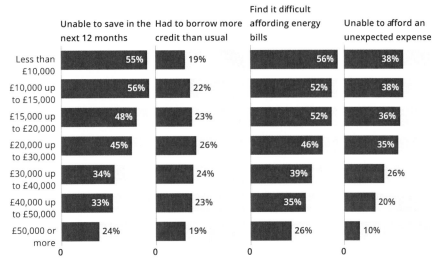

Source: Office for National Statistics (ONS) – Opinions and Lifestyle Survey (OPN)

Notes:

1. "Find it difficult affording energy bills" is among adults who were responsible for paying energy bills.

Download the data

.xlsx (https://www.ons.gov.uk/visualisations/dvc2479/fig6/datadownload.xlsx)

Housing tenure

After controlling for a range of characteristics, renters had over four times the odds of experiencing some form of financial vulnerability (odds ratio equals 4.4) when compared with those who own their home outright. Adults in all other housing tenure groups also had higher odds and were therefore more likely to experience some form of financial vulnerability when compared with homeowners.

Figure 7: Renters had over four times the odds of experiencing some form of financial vulnerability, compared with those who own their home outright

Great Britain, September 2022 to January 2023

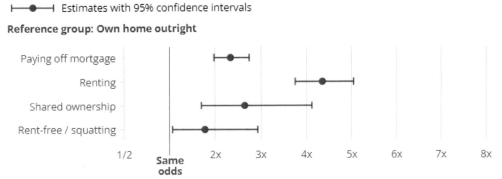

Source: Office for National Statistics (ONS) – Opinions and Lifestyle Survey (OPN)

Notes:

1. An odds ratio indicates the likelihood of experiencing some form of financial vulnerability given a particular characteristic.

Download the data

.xlsx (https://www.ons.gov.uk/visualisations/dvc2479/fig7/datadownload.xlsx)

When looking at the measures that contribute to financial vulnerability, we found that:

- adults renting their home were over four times more likely to report being unable to afford an unexpected expense of £850 (55%), compared with those who own their home outright (12%), and around twice as likely compared with those who are paying off a mortgage (28%)

- renters were also more likely to report borrowing more money or using more credit than usual compared with a year ago (31%), compared with outright homeowners (9%) and those paying off a mortgage (25%)

- a higher proportion of adults who rent their home reported being unable to save in the next 12 months (56%), compared with those who own their home outright (38%) and those who are paying off a mortgage (40%)

- finding it difficult affording energy bills was also more common for renters who are responsible for paying these bills (61%) compared with outright homeowners (32%) and those with a mortgage (44%)

Figure 8: Adults who rent their home were almost five times more likely to report being unable to afford an unexpected expense of £850, compared with those who own their home outright

Proportion of people reporting factors contributing to financial vulnerability by housing tenure, Great Britain, September 2022 to January 2023

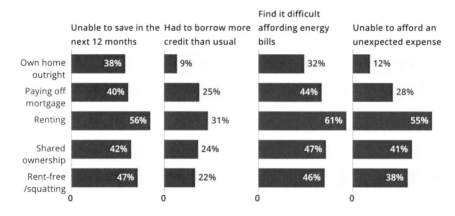

Source: Office for National Statistics (ONS) – Opinions and Lifestyle Survey (OPN)

Notes:

1. "Find it difficult affording energy bills" is among adults who were responsible for paying energy bills.

Download the data

.xlsx (https://www.ons.gov.uk/visualisations/dvc2479/fig8/datadownload.xlsx)

Parental status

After controlling for a range of characteristics, parents living with dependent children aged 5 years and over had odds four times higher of experiencing some form of financial vulnerability (odds ratio equals 4.1) than non-parents or parents not living with dependent children. Parents living with younger dependent children had odds three times higher (odds ratio equals 3.5).

Figure 9: Parents living with dependent children had higher odds of experiencing some form of financial vulnerability, compared with non-parents or parents not living with dependent children

Great Britain, September 2022 to January 2023

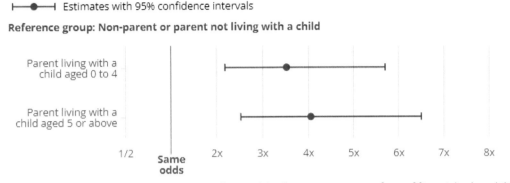

Source: Office for National Statistics (ONS) – Opinions and Lifestyle Survey (OPN)

Notes:

1. An odds ratio indicates the likelihood of experiencing some form of financial vulnerability given a particular characteristic.

2. Living with a child refers to living with a dependent child. For further information, see the Glossary. (https://www.ons.gov.uk/peoplepopulationandcommunity/personalandhouseholdfinances/expenditure/articles/impactofincreasedcostoflivingonadultsacrossgreatbritain/september2022tojanuary2023#glossary)

Download the data

.xlsx (https://www.ons.gov.uk/visualisations/dvc2479/fig9/datadownload.xlsx)

When looking at the measures that contribute to financial vulnerability, we found that:

- being unable to afford an unexpected expense of £850 was most commonly reported by parents living with a dependent child aged 0 to 4 years (47%) and aged 5 years or over (42%), compared with just over a quarter (28%) of non-parents or parents not living with a dependent child

- parents living with a dependent child aged 0 to 4 years and aged 5 years or over were more likely to report borrowing more money or using more credit than usual compared with a year ago (36% and 34%, respectively), compared with non-parents or parents not living with a dependent child (18%)

- a higher proportion of parents living with a dependent child aged 0 to 4 years and aged 5 years or over reported being unable to save in the next 12 months (56% and 53% respectively), compared with 42% of non-parents or parents not living with a dependent child

- parents living with a dependent child aged 0 to 4 years and aged 5 years or over who were responsible for paying energy bills were more likely to report finding it difficult affording them (58% and 56%, respectively), when compared with non-parents or parents no living with dependent child (42%)

Figure 10: More than half of parents living with a dependent child reported being unable to save in the next 12 months (54%), compared with 42% of non-parents or parents not living with a dependent child

Proportion of people reporting factors contributing to financial vulnerability by parental status, Great Britain, September 2022 to January 2023

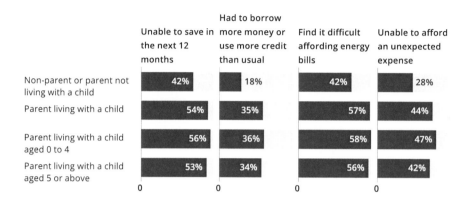

Source: Office for National Statistics (ONS) – Opinions and Lifestyle Survey (OPN)

Notes:

1. Living with a child refers to living with a dependent child. Parent living with a dependent child has been split into two further groups: parent living with a dependent child aged 0 to 4 years and parent living with a dependent child aged 5 years and over. For further information, see the Glossary. (https://www.ons.gov.uk/peoplepopulationandcommunity/personalandhouseholdfinances/expenditure/articles/impactofincreasedcostoflivingonadultsacrossgreatbritain/september2022tojanuary2023#glossary)

2. "Find it difficult affording energy bills" is among adults who were responsible for paying energy bills.

Download the data

.xlsx (https://www.ons.gov.uk/visualisations/dvc2479/fig10/datadownload.xlsx)

4. Impact of increased cost of living on adults across Great Britain data

Impact of increased cost of living on adults across Great Britain (https://www.ons.gov.uk/peoplepopulationandcommunity/personalandhouseholdfinances/expenditure/datasets/impactofincreasedcostoflivingonadultsacrossgreatbritain)

Dataset | Released 20 February 2023

Proportion of the population that are affected by an increase in their cost of living and the individual characteristics associated with financial vulnerability.

Debt and well-being in Great Britain (https://www.ons.gov.uk/peoplepopulationandcommunity/wellbeing/datasets/financialpressuresandwellbeingingreatbritaindata)

Dataset | Released 22 February 2022

Data exploring the financial situations of adults in Great Britain from the Opinions and Lifestyle Survey, broken down by well-being and loneliness.

5. Glossary

Area deprivation

Area deprivation is represented by the Index of Multiple Deprivation (IMD) and is the official measure of relative deprivation for small areas in England. The IMD ranks every small area in England from 1 (most deprived area) to 32,844 (least deprived area). Deciles are calculated by ranking the 32,844 small areas in England, from most deprived to least deprived, and dividing them into 10 equal groups. These range from the most deprived 10 percent of small areas nationally to the least deprived 10 percent of small areas nationally. To ensure robust sample sizes, we have further grouped deciles into quintiles.

Logistic regression

We carried out a logistic regression analysis to identify the individual characteristics associated with financial vulnerability. This further allows us to identify someone with a particular characteristic having higher or lower odds of experiencing some form of financial vulnerability when compared with a specified reference group, after taking other possible characteristics into account.

For example, if a particular group has an odds ratio of more than one, they are more likely than the reference group to be considered financially vulnerable when compared with the reference group.

Odds ratio

An odds ratio indicates the likelihood of experiencing some form of financial vulnerability given a particular characteristic. When a characteristic has an odds ratio of one, this means there is neither an increase nor a decrease in the likelihood of experiencing some form of financial vulnerability compared with the reference category. An odds ratio greater than one indicates an increased likelihood of experiencing some form of financial vulnerability compared with the reference category. An odds ratio less than one indicates a decreased likelihood of experiencing some form of financial vulnerability compared with the reference category.

Parental status

An adult is defined as a parent if they are the parent of a dependent child living in the household. Dependent children in this case includes children and stepchildren.

Parents were classified into two further groups; having a dependent child aged under 5 years or having a dependent child aged 5 years and over living in the household. Where parents have multiple dependent children in their household, they are included in a group based on the age of their youngest dependent child in their household. A dependent child is someone aged under 16 years or someone who is aged 16 to 18 years, has never been married and is in full-time education.

Personal annual income

Personal annual gross income is self-reported on the Opinions and Lifestyle Survey (OPN) and therefore should be treated with caution. A respondent's income information does not represent equivalised household income, that considers that households with more people will need a higher income to achieve the same standard of living as households with fewer members.

Prepayment meter user

A person has been assigned to the category "Pay for gas and/or electricity using top up prepayments" if they reported they had gas and electricity supplied to their home and they topped up a meter using a key, card or app for their gas and/or electricity.

A person has been assigned to the category "Do not pay for gas and electricity using top up prepayments" if they reported they had gas and electricity supplied to their home, had not indicated they paid using a key, card or app for their gas or electricity and indicated they paid by either direct debit or one-off bill payments for either their gas and electricity.

For anyone who indicated that they paid for their gas and electricity in one payment, it is assumed that using a prepayment meter is not possible.

Statistical significance

This article presents a summary of results, with further data including confidence intervals (https://www.ons.gov.uk/methodology/methodologytopicsandstatisticalconcepts/uncertaintyandhowwemeasureit#confidence-interval) for the estimates shown in the charts presented contained in the associated datasets. Where comparisons between groups are presented, 95% confidence intervals should be used to assess the statistical significance (https://www.ons.gov.uk/methodology/methodologytopicsandstatisticalconcepts/uncertaintyandhowwemeasureit#statistical-significance) of the change.

For the regression analysis, characteristics were found to be significant based on the p-value associated (Wald Chi-Squared Test) with each characteristic. The odds ratios were then assessed alongside a confidence interval around each category of interest.

6. Data sources and quality

Comparing over time

Changes were made to the survey methodology in the latest pooled period, 14 September 2022 to 8 January 2023; therefore, we do not recommend making comparisons with previous pooled periods. Any differences should be treated with caution.

Quality

More quality and methodology information on the Opinions and Lifestyle Survey (OPN) and its strengths, limitations, appropriate uses, and how the data were created is available in our Opinions and Lifestyle Survey Quality and Methodology Information (https://www.ons.gov.uk/peoplepopulationandcommunity/healthandsocialcare/healthandlifeexpectancies/methodologies/opinionsandlifestylesurveyqmi).

Regression analysis

The analysis from the regression model presented in this article identifies differences between adults who were considered to be financially vulnerable (dependent variable), when compared with adults not considered to be financially vulnerable, while controlling for a range of characteristics (independent variables).

Three logistic regression models were produced to explain the relationships between the dependent and independent variables. These were:

- unadjusted: these models show the relationship between the dependent variable, and an independent variable of interest (characteristic)

- age and sex adjusted: these models looked at the same dependent and independent variables of interest while also controlling for age and sex

- fully adjusted: these models looked at the same dependent variable and a range of independent variables (characteristics) of interest while controlling for all variables

Missing values were excluded from the regression analysis where a response was not provided for a question or variable included in the model. As a result, 18,300 adults were included in the fully-adjusted regression model analysis.

The results of the modelling and a full breakdown of sample sizes and population estimates for each of the characteristics included in the fully adjusted regression model are available in the accompanying dataset. (https://www.ons.gov.uk/peoplepopulationandcommunity/personalandhouseholdfinances/expenditure/datasets/impactofincreasedcostoflivingonadultsacrossgreatbritain)

Sampling

The analysis throughout this article is based on adults aged 16 years and over in Great Britain. The analysis in this report is based on 18,464 adults from a pooled dataset comprising eight waves of data collection, covering the following periods:

- 14 to 25 September 2022

- 29 September to 9 October 2022

- 12 to 23 October 2022

- 26 October to 6 November 2022

- 8 to 20 November 2022

- 22 November to 4 December 2022

- 7 to 18 December 2022

- 21 December to 8 January 2023

Further information on the survey design and quality can be found in our <u>Opinions and Lifestyle Survey Quality and Methodology</u> <u>Information</u>
<u>(https://www.ons.gov.uk/peoplepopulationandcommunity/healthandsocialcare/healthandlifeexpectancies/methodologies/opinionsandlifesty</u> <u>lesurveyqmi</u>).

Weighting

Survey weights were applied to make estimates representative of the population.

Weights were first adjusted for non-response and attrition. Subsequently, the weights were calibrated to satisfy population distributions considering the following factors: sex by age, region, tenure, highest qualification and employment status.

For age, sex and region, population totals based on projections of mid-year population estimates for June 2021 were used. The resulting weighted sample is therefore representative of the Great Britain adult population by a number of socio-demographic factors and geography.

7. Related links

The cost of living, current and upcoming work: February 2023

(https://www.ons.gov.uk/economy/inflationandpriceindices/articles/thecostoflivingcurrentandupcomingwork/february2023)

Article | Released 8 February 2023

A summary of our current and future analytical work related to the cost of living.

Characteristics of adults experiencing energy and food insecurity in Great Britain: 22 November to 18 December 2022

(https://www.ons.gov.uk/peoplepopulationandcommunity/wellbeing/articles/characteristicsofadultsexperiencingenergyandfoodinsecurit
ygreatbritain/22novemberto18december2022)

Article | Released 13 February 2023

Understanding the characteristics associated with experiencing energy and food insecurity; logistic regression analysis using data from the Winter Survey.

Impact of increased cost of living on adults across Great Britain: June to September 2022

(https://www.ons.gov.uk/peoplepopulationandcommunity/personalandhouseholdfinances/expenditure/articles/impactofincreasedcosto
flivingonadultsacrossgreatbritain/junetoseptember2022)

Article | Released 25 October 2022

Analysis of the proportion of the population that are affected by an increase in their cost of living, and of the characteristics associated with having difficulty affording or being behind on energy, mortgage or rental payments, using data from the Opinions and Lifestyle Survey.

Public opinions and social trends, Great Britain: 25 January to 5 February 2023

(https://www.ons.gov.uk/peoplepopulationandcommunity/wellbeing/bulletins/publicopinionsandsocialtrendsgreatbritain/25januaryto5f
ebruary2023)

Bulletin | Released 10 February 2023

Social insights on daily life and events, including the cost of living, working arrangements and well-being from the Opinions and Lifestyle Survey (OPN).

Cost of living latest insights (https://www.ons.gov.uk/economy/inflationandpriceindices/articles/costofliving/latestinsights)

Insights tool | Updated daily

The latest data and trends about the cost of living. Explore changes in the cost of everyday items and how this is affecting people.

The impact of winter pressures on adults in Great Britain: December 2022

(https://www.ons.gov.uk/peoplepopulationandcommunity/wellbeing/articles/theimpactofwinterpressuresonadultsingreatbritain/decem
ber2022)

Article | Released 15 December 2022

First insights from our new winter survey providing monthly updates on how increases in the cost of living and difficulty accessing NHS services are impacting people's lives during the autumn and winter months.

8. Cite this article

Office for National Statistics (ONS), released 20 February 2023, ONS website, article, Impact of increased cost of living on adults across Great Britain: September 2022 to January 2023

(https://www.ons.gov.uk/peoplepopulationandcommunity/personalandhouseholdfinances/expenditure/articles/impactofincreasedcosto
flivingonadultsacrossgreatbritain/september2022tojanuary2023)

Contact details for this article

Jodie Davis, Unity Amoaku, Simeon North, Henry Beevor and Tim Vizard
policy.evidence.analysis@ons.gov.uk
Telephone: +44 300 0671543

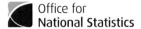

<u>Data and analysis from Census 2021</u>

Impact of increased cost of living on adults across Great Britain: February to May 2023

Analysis of the proportion of the population that are affected by an increase in their cost of living, and of the characteristics associated with financial vulnerability, using data from the Opinions and Lifestyle survey.

Contact:
Lili Chowdhury, Caleb Ogwuru, Chris Jones, David Ainslie and Tim Vizard

Release date:
14 July 2023

Table of contents

1. Main points

In this article, we have identified groups of the population experiencing financial vulnerability in Great Britain. In the period, 8 February to 1 May 2023, using the Opinions and Lifestyle Survey (OPN), we found:

- renters (4.7 higher odds) and mortgage holders (2.0 higher odds) had higher odds of experiencing financial vulnerability compared with those who own their home outright

- the difference between renters' and mortgage holders' likelihood of experiencing some form of financial vulnerability may reflect that, on average, renters report spending a higher proportion of their disposable income on rent (21%), than mortgage holders on their mortgage (16%), according to the latest data from the Living Cost and Food Survey (UK, financial year ending 2022)

- other groups with higher odds of experiencing financial vulnerability included adults aged 25 to 34 years (3.4 higher odds compared with those aged 75 years and over) and disabled adults (1.9 higher odds compared with non-disabled adults)

Examining groups of the population who were having difficulty with their rent, mortgage or affording food shopping specifically, we found:

- around a third (35%) of adults reported it was difficult (very or somewhat) to afford their rent or mortgage payments, this proportion appeared higher among groups including; those receiving support from charities (57%), living in a household with one adult and at least one child (47%), receiving some form of benefits or financial support (45%), Asian or Asian British adults (53%), Black, African, Caribbean or Black British adults (47%), renters (43%) and disabled adults (41%)

- around 4 in 10 (43%) renters reported that it was difficult to afford their rent payments, and around 3 in 10 (28%) mortgage holders reported it was difficult to afford their mortgage payments

- around 1 in 20 (5%) of adults reported that in the past two weeks they had ran out of food and had been unable to afford more, this proportion appeared higher among groups including; those receiving support from charities (45%), living in a household with one adult and at least one child (28%), receiving some form of benefits or financial support (21%), Mixed or Multiple ethnicity adults (14%), Black, African, Caribbean or Black British adults (13%), renters (14%) and disabled adults (9%)

2. Experiences of increased cost of living

Our latest Public opinions and social trends, Great Britain bulletin
(https://www.ons.gov.uk/peoplepopulationandcommunity/wellbeing/bulletins/publicopinionsandsocialtrendsgreatbritain/28juneto9july2023
) reported that, during the period 28 June to 9 July 2023, around 9 in 10 adults (92%) see the cost of living as an important issue facing the
UK. Around 6 in 10 (60%) adults reported that their cost of living had increased compared with a month ago.

Commonly reported reasons among adults who said their cost of living had increased compared with a month ago continue to be an
increase in:

- the price of food shopping (96%)
- gas or electricity bills (57%)
- the price of fuel (37%)
- rent or mortgage costs (27%)

These reported experiences reflect our inflation data, which shows that food and non-alcoholic beverage prices rose by 18.4%, in the year to
May 2023 (Figure 1). For further information about our inflation data, see our Consumer price inflation, UK: May 2023 bulletin
(https://www.ons.gov.uk/economy/inflationandpriceindices/bulletins/consumerpriceinflation/may2023).

Figure 1: Annual inflation rates by selected divisions

Annual inflation rates by selected divisions, UK, May 2013 to May 2023

Source: Consumer price inflation from the Office for National Statistics

Throughout the rest of this article, we have used a larger pooled dataset covering 8 February to 1 May 2023 (the "latest pooled period"), to
explore how the rising cost of living is impacting different groups of the population. This article highlights some of these differences,
however further data can be found in the accompanying dataset
(https://www.ons.gov.uk/peoplepopulationandcommunity/personalandhouseholdfinances/expenditure/datasets/impactofincreasedcostolivi
ngonadultsacrossgreatbritain).

Survey respondents were asked: "Finally, in your own words, tell us about your experiences with the increases in cost of living." We use
quotes from responses to this question to illustrate our findings throughout this article. Quotes are sometimes shortened, as indicated by
[...], to enable ease of reading. The underlying meaning of the quote remains the same. Information about further analysis of these
responses is available in Section 6: Lived experience of increases in the cost of living
(https://www.ons.gov.uk/peoplepopulationandcommunity/personalandhouseholdfinances/expenditure/articles/impactofincreasedcostoflivin

gonadultsacrossgreatbritain/februarytomay2023#lived-experience-of-increases-in-the-cost-of-living) and Section 9: Data sources and quality (https://www.ons.gov.uk/peoplepopulationandcommunity/personalandhouseholdfinances/expenditure/articles/impactofincreasedcostoflivingonadultsacrossgreatbritain/februarytomay2023#data-sources-and-quality).

3. Financial vulnerability

> "With rising costs in rent and energy we have decided to move home to a smaller place [...] the creeping cost of living has taken its toll on us in a big way [...]"

We identified groups of the population who were more likely to be experiencing financial vulnerability.

A person was considered to be experiencing financial vulnerability if three or more of the following applied to them:

- being unable to afford an unexpected, but necessary, expense of £850

- borrowing more money or using more credit than usual, in the last month, compared with a year ago

- being unable to save in the next 12 months

- finding it very or somewhat difficult to afford energy bills

Figure 2 shows trends over time in the proportion of adults reporting each of these.

Figure 2: Measures of financial vulnerability are relatively stable in 2023

Great Britain, 3 November 2021 to 9 July 2023

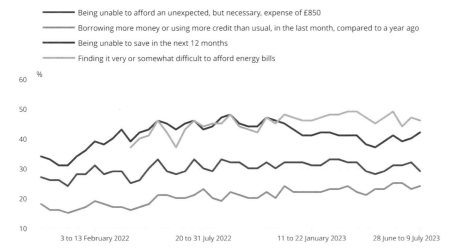

Source: Opinions and Lifestyle Survey from the Office for National Statistics

Notes:

1. Questions: 1. "Could your household afford to pay an unexpected, but necessary, expense of £850?"; 2. "Have you had to borrow more money or use more credit than usual in the last month, compared to a year ago?"; 3. "In view of the general economic situation, do you think you will be able to save any money in the next 12 months"; 4. "How easy or difficult is it to afford your energy bills?".

2. Base: Question 1, 2 and 3 equals all adults. Question 4 equals adults who pay energy bills.

3. Estimates for question 4 are not available for the period 3 November to 27 March, as the question was not asked in this period.

Around a quarter (24%) of all adults were experiencing some form of financial vulnerability in the latest pooled period, a similar proportion to the period September 2022 to January 2023 (23%).

We conducted a logistic regression analysis that assessed the likelihood of experiencing financial vulnerability, after controlling for a variety of personal characteristics.

This analysis technique helps account for an individual groups pattern of other characteristics. For example, those who own their homes tend to be older, have higher incomes, and live in smaller household sizes, according to the latest data from the English Housing Survey 2021 to 2022: headline report (https://www.gov.uk/government/statistics/english-housing-survey-2021-to-2022-headline-report/english-housing-survey-2021-to-2022-headline-report).

We found that the groups of the population with the highest odds of being financially vulnerable in the latest pooled period remained similar to the period September 2022 to January 2023, as shown in our Impact of increased cost of living on adults across Great Britain bulletin (https://www.ons.gov.uk/peoplepopulationandcommunity/personalandhouseholdfinances/expenditure/articles/impactofincreasedcostofliving onadultsacrossgreatbritain/september2022tojanuary2023). These included:

- renters (4.7 higher odds) and mortgage holders (2.0 higher odds), who had higher odds of experiencing financial vulnerability, compared with those who own their home outright

- adults with a personal annual income of up to £10,000, who had higher odds of experiencing financial vulnerability (3.8 higher odds), compared with adults earning £50,000 or more per year

- adults aged 25 to 34 years, who had higher odds of experiencing financial vulnerability (3.4 higher odds), compared with those aged 75 years and over

- disabled adults, who had higher odds of experiencing financial vulnerability (1.9 higher odds), compared with non-disabled adults

Figure 3: Renters had around five times the odds of experiencing some form of financial vulnerability, compared with those who own their home outright

Great Britain, 8 February to 1 May 2023

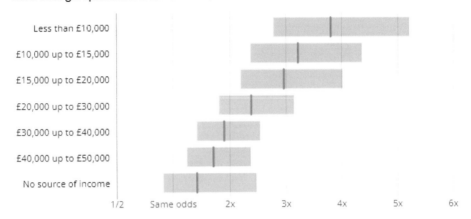

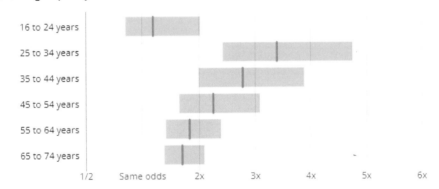

Source: Opinions and Lifestyle Survey from the Office for National Statistics

Notes:

1. An odds ratio indicates the likelihood of experiencing some form of financial vulnerability given a particular characteristic.

2. Confidence intervals may appear to be unequal because of rounding.

Download the data

.xlsx (https://www.ons.gov.uk/visualisations/dvc2642/fig3/datadownload.xlsx)

Estimates for other groups of the population considered are available in the accompanying dataset (https://www.ons.gov.uk/peoplepopulationandcommunity/personalandhouseholdfinances/expenditure/datasets/impactofincreasedcostoflivingonadultsacrossgreatbritain). For more information on the regression analysis, see Section 9: Data sources and quality (https://www.ons.gov.uk/peoplepopulationandcommunity/personalandhouseholdfinances/expenditure/articles/impactofincreasedcostoflivingonadultsacrossgreatbritain/februarytomay2023#data-sources-and-quality).

4. Rent and mortgages

> "I have friends and family who are struggling with finding housing to rent that they can afford. A couple of close friends are beginning to feel very tired [...] unwell and are at pension age but cannot afford to reduce their working hours. Younger people I know are struggling badly to find housing [...]"

Our latest Public opinions and social trends, Great Britain: 28 June to 9 July 2023 bulletin (https://www.ons.gov.uk/releases/publicopinionsandsocialtrendsgreatbritain28juneto9july2023) shows that around half of adults (48%) who currently pay rent or a mortgage reported that their payments had increased in the last six months. This proportion has gradually increased since February 2023.

Figure 4: The proportion of adults reporting their rent or mortgage payments have increased in the last six months has gradually increased since February 2023

Proportion among adults who are currently paying rent or mortgage, Great Britain, 16 March 2022 to 9 July 2023

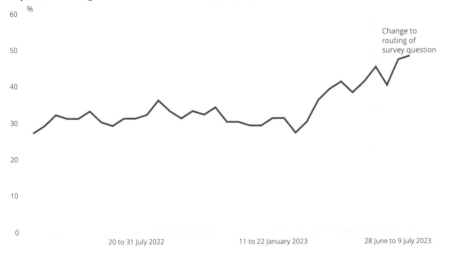

Source: Opinions and Lifestyle Survey from the Office for National Statistics

Notes:

1. Question: "Have your rent or mortgage payments gone up in the last 6 months?".

2. Base: adults who are currently paying rent or mortgage.

3. Changes were made to survey design to allow us to more accurately route to the questions on rent and mortgage payments. Because of this there is a break in the time series from the period 17 to 29 May 2023.

In the latest pooled period, we found that those renting (42%) were more likely to report an increase in their payments than mortgage holders (32%).

According to data from our Index of Private Housing Rental Prices, UK: May 2023 bulletin (https://www.ons.gov.uk/economy/inflationandpriceindices/bulletins/indexofprivatehousingrentalprices/may2023), private rental prices paid by tenants in the UK increased by 5.0% in the 12 months to May 2023. This represents the largest annual percentage change since this UK series began in January 2016.

While interest rates have been increasing since the start of 2022, as shown on the Interest rates and Bank rate webpage from the Bank of England (https://www.bankofengland.co.uk/monetary-policy/the-interest-rate-bank-rate), many fixed rate mortgage borrowers have so far been insulated from these increases. Analysis of Bank of England data in our How increases in housing costs impact households article (https://www.ons.gov.uk/peoplepopulationandcommunity/housing/articles/howincreasesinhousingcostsimpacthouseholds/2023-01-09), shows that most mortgages are agreed at a fixed interest rate, where the interest rates stay the same for the duration of the mortgage deal. Around 9 in 10 (88%) outstanding UK mortgages were being repaid through fixed interest rate mortgages in Quarter 1 (Jan to Mar) 2023.

Difficulty affording rent or mortgage payments

Groups of the population who were more likely to report finding it very or somewhat difficult to afford their rent or mortgage payments in the latest pooled period included:

- around 4 in 10 (43%) renters, compared with 28% of mortgage holders

- around 4 in 10 among adults within the lowest four quintiles of annual personal income (39% in the lowest quintile, 41% in the second, 38% in the third, 38% in the fourth), compared with 26% of those in the fifth and highest quintile (for more information on personal annual income quintiles, see Section 8: Glossary (https://www.ons.gov.uk/peoplepopulationandcommunity/personalandhouseholdfinances/expenditure/articles/impactofincreasedcosto flivingonadultsacrossgreatbritain/februarytomay2023#glossary))

- around 4 in 10 (41%) among disabled adults, compared with 32% of non-disabled adults

- around 6 in 10 (57%) among adults who report receiving support from charities, including foodbanks, because of increases in their cost of living, compared with 34% among adults who do not receive support from charities

- around half (47%) among adults living in a household with one adult and at least one dependent child, compared with 36% among adults living in a household with more than one adult and at least one dependent child and 34% among adults not living with a dependent child

- over 4 in 10 (45%) among adults receiving some form of benefit or financial support (for more information on the definition of this group, see Section 8: Glossary (https://www.ons.gov.uk/peoplepopulationandcommunity/personalandhouseholdfinances/expenditure/articles/impactofincreasedcosto flivingonadultsacrossgreatbritain/februarytomay2023#glossary)), compared with 33% among adults who were not

- around half among Asian or Asian British adults (53%) or Black, African, Caribbean or Black British adults (47%), compared with 33% among White adults

Estimates among all adults and by a selection of personal characteristics considered in this analysis are shown in Figure 5.

Figure 5: Difficulty affording rent or mortgage payments among different groups of the population

Proportion of adults finding it somewhat or very difficult to afford rent or mortgage payments, Great Britain, 8 February to 1 May 2023

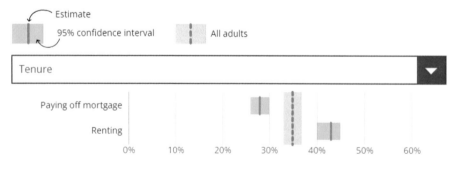

Source: Opinions and Lifestyle Survey from the Office for National Statistics

Note: This is a snapshot of an interactive image, to view the full image please go to: https://www.ons.gov.uk/peoplepopulationandcommunity/personalandhouseholdfinances/expenditure/articles/impactofincreasedcostoflivingonadultsacrossgreatbritain/februarytomay2023

Notes:

1. Question: "How easy or difficult is it to afford your rent or mortgage payments?".

2. Base: adults who are currently paying rent or mortgage.

3. Confidence intervals may appear to be unequal because of rounding.

4. Parental status categories are not mutually exclusive.

Download the data

.xlsx (https://www.ons.gov.uk/visualisations/dvc2642/fig5/datadownload.xlsx)

Impact of cost of living increases on renters

New analysis from the Living Cost and Food (LCF) survey for the financial year ending 2022 reflects some of the reasons why renters might currently report more difficulty than mortgage holders. The analysis showed that renters (21%) spent a higher proportion of their average weekly disposable income on housing costs (rent or mortgage) compared with mortgage holders (16%). These estimates and how they varied among renters and mortgage holders by age group, sex and income are available in the accompanying dataset (https://www.ons.gov.uk/peoplepopulationandcommunity/personalandhouseholdfinances/expenditure/datasets/expenditureonmortgagean drentasaproportionoftotalexpenditureanddisposableincomeuk).

Analysis of the latest pooled period (8 February to 1 May 2023) of the Opinions and Lifestyle Survey (OPN) survey suggests spending a higher proportion of disposable income on housing costs could be affectcting the ability of renters to afford other essential costs.

Adults renting were more likely than mortgage holders to report:

- spending less on food shopping and essentials (58% of renters, compared with 48% of mortgage holders)

- running out of food in the past two weeks (14%, compared with 3%)

- being behind on gas or electricity payments (13%, compared with 4%)

- having a direct debit or standing order that they have been unable to pay in the past month (19%, compared with 4%)

- using support from charities (8%, compared with 1%)

Adults renting were less likely than mortgage holders to report that they:

- will be able to save any money in the next 12 months (26%, compared with 48% of mortgage holders)

- were using savings because of increases in the cost of living (22%, compared with 29%)

Estimates from the latest pooled period by these and all other personal characteristics considered in this analysis (including employment status, highest education level, the country and region, urban or rural nature, or level of deprivation of the area in which adults live) can be found in the accompanying dataset (https://www.ons.gov.uk/peoplepopulationandcommunity/personalandhouseholdfinances/expenditure/datasets/impactofincreasedcostoflivi ngonadultsacrossgreatbritain).

5. Impact of increases in the price of food

> "[...] the rising cost of food has meant that we have had to amend our shopping habits and we rarely go [...] shopping [...] the rising cost of energy has meant that we rarely have the heating on so we wear warm clothing and lots of layers [...]"

Pressures on cost of living from food prices remain, our latest Public opinions and social trends, Great Britain: 28 June to 9 July 2023 bulletin (https://www.ons.gov.uk/peoplepopulationandcommunity/wellbeing/bulletins/publicopinionsandsocialtrendsgreatbritain/28juneto9july2023) shows that among all adults the most commonly reported reason for an increase in cost of living, compared with a month ago, is an increase in the price of food shopping (96%).

This latest data also shows that around half of adults reported spending more than usual to get what they usually buy (45%) or buying less food (48%) in the last two weeks. Around 1 in 20 (5%) reported they or their household had run out of food and not been able to afford more.

These proportions appear relatively stable during 2023 (Figure 6), this may be because of other changes in behaviour as adults adapt to consistently high prices. For example, there is evidence that consumers have been changing to cheaper supermarket own-brand products, with total spending on value range products increasing 41% in the past year, as shown in Kantars release on grocery price inflation (https://www.kantar.com/uki/inspiration/fmcg/2023-wp-uk-grocery-inflation-falls-but-shoppers-still-feeling-the-pressure).

High food prices may also impact people's ability to afford healthy choices. The Food Foundation (https://foodfoundation.org.uk/publication/broken-plate-2023) reported that the most deprived fifth of the population need to spend 50% of their disposable income on food to meet the cost of the Government recommended healthy diet, compared with 11% among the least deprived fifth.

Figure 6: Around 1 in 20 adults continue to report running out of food and being unable to afford to buy more

Among all adults, Great Britain, 8 September 2021 to 9 July 2023

Source: Opinions and Lifestyle Survey from the Office for National Statistics

Notes:

1. Questions: 1. "In the past two weeks, have you experienced any of the following when food shopping?"; 2. "In the past two weeks, which, if any, have you been doing when food shopping?"; 3. "In the past two weeks, have you or your household run out of food and could not afford to buy more?".

2. Base: all adults.

3. Respondents were able to choose more than one response for question 1.

4. Estimates for question 1 and 3 are not available for the period 8 September to 17 October and 8 September to 20 November, respectively, as the questions were not asked in these periods.

Using the latest pooled period to examine this further, groups of the population who were more likely to report that in the past two weeks they or their household had run out of food and not been able to afford to buy more included:

- around 1 in 7 (14%) renters, compared with 3% of mortgage holders

- around 1 in 10 (9%) among adults in the lowest quintile of annual personal income (7% in the second, 6% in the third, 4% in the fourth), compared with 1% of those in the fifth and highest quintile

- around 1 in 10 (9%) among disabled adults, compared with 4% of non-disabled adults

- around half (45%) among adults who report receiving support from charities because of increases in their cost of living, compared with 4% among adults who do not

- around a quarter (28%) among adults living in a household with one adult and at least one dependent child, compared with 7% among adults living in a household with more than one adult and at least one dependent child and 4% among adults not living with a dependent child

- around 1 in 5 (21%) among adults receiving some form of benefit or financial support, compared with 3% among adults who were not (for more information on the definition of this group, see Section 8: Glossary (https://www.ons.gov.uk/peoplepopulationandcommunity/personalandhouseholdfinances/expenditure/articles/impactofincreasedcosto flivingonadultsacrossgreatbritain/februarytomay2023#glossary))

- around 1 in 7 among Black, African, Caribbean or Black British adults (13%) or Mixed or Multiple ethnic group adults (14%), compared with 5% among White adults and 6% among Asian or Asian British adults.

Figure 7: Running out of food and being unable to afford more among different groups of the population

Proportion of adults who report running out of food, in the past two weeks, and being unable to afford to buy more, Great Britain, 8 February to 1 May 2023

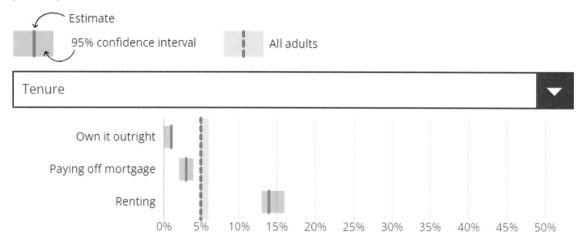

Source: Opinions and Lifestyle Survey from the Office for National Statistics

Note: This is a snapshot of an interactive image, to view the full image please go to: https://www.ons.gov.uk/peoplepopulationandcommunity/personalandhouseholdfinances/expenditure/articles/impactofincreasedcostoflivingonadultsacrossgreatbritain/februarytomay2023

Notes:

1. Question: "In the past two weeks, have you or your household run out of food and could not afford to buy more?".

2. Base: all adults.

3. Confidence intervals may appear to be unequal because of rounding.

4. Parental status categories are not mutually exclusive.

Download the data

.xlsx (https://www.ons.gov.uk/visualisations/dvc2642/fig7/datadownload.xlsx)

Although around half of all adults (50%) reported buying less than usual in the past two weeks, some groups of the population were less likely to report taking this action. This included those:

- in the highest quintile of personal income (41%)

- aged 70 years and above (35%)

- who owned their home outright (37%)

Estimates regarding people's experiences when food shopping by all personal characteristics considered in this analysis (also including employment status, highest education level, the country and region, urban or rural nature, or level of deprivation of the area in which adults live) can be found in the accompanying dataset (https://www.ons.gov.uk/peoplepopulationandcommunity/personalandhouseholdfinances/expenditure/datasets/impactofincreasedcostoflivingonadultsacrossgreatbritain).

6. Lived experience of increases in the cost of living

Between 19 April and 1 May 2023, survey respondents were asked; "Finally, in your own words, tell us about your experiences with the increases in cost of living." Quotes used throughout this article highlight responses that relate to the quantitative findings shown.

Using Natural Language Processing (NLP) (see Section 8: Data sources and quality (https://www.ons.gov.uk/peoplepopulationandcommunity/personalandhouseholdfinances/expenditure/articles/impactofincreasedcostoflivingonadultsacrossgreatbritain/februarytomay2023#glossary)), we identified five overarching themes, which highlight the perceptions and lived experience respondents had of the rising cost of living.

"Well-being and worries about the future"

Respondents described issues relating to personal well-being and their worries about the future considering the rising cost of living, which was described in terms of a drain on energy and vitality, dominating every-day conversations in a negative way, and having a mental health impact.

"Response by government and businesses"

Respondents described concerns related to companies making profit despite the rises in the cost of living and raised questions regarding the government's response.

"Worry about others"

Respondents expressed a range of worries about both people close to them or in the general population.

"Shopping habits"

Respondents described changes to their shopping habits and behaviours in response to the increases in the cost of living, such as:

- shopping less
- wearing warm clothing instead of turning the heating on
- spending less on non-essentials
- shopping around

"Widening inequality"

Respondents described their perceptions of growing inequalities and their sentiments regarding this.

The themes resulting from this initial qualitative analysis will be used to guide future analysis in our Impact of increased cost of living on adults across Great Britain series (https://www.ons.gov.uk/peoplepopulationandcommunity/personalandhouseholdfinances/expenditure/articles/impactofincreasedcostoflivingonadultsacrossgreatbritain/previousReleases). For more information about these themes, see Section 9: Data sources and quality (https://www.ons.gov.uk/peoplepopulationandcommunity/personalandhouseholdfinances/expenditure/articles/impactofincreasedcostoflivingonadultsacrossgreatbritain/februarytomay2023#data-sources-and-quality).

7. Impact of increased cost of living on adults across Great Britain data

Impact of increased cost of living on adults across Great Britain
(https://www.ons.gov.uk/peoplepopulationandcommunity/personalandhouseholdfinances/expenditure/datasets/impactofincreasedcost
oflivingonadultsacrossgreatbritain)
Dataset | Released 14 July 2023
People in Great Britain's experiences of and actions following increases in their costs of living, and how these differed by a range of
personal characteristics

Expenditure on mortgage and rent as a proportion of total expenditure and disposable income, UK
(https://www.ons.gov.uk/peoplepopulationandcommunity/personalandhouseholdfinances/expenditure/datasets/expenditureonmortga
geandrentasaproportionoftotalexpenditureanddisposableincomeuk)
Dataset | Released 14 July 2023
Expenditure on rent by renters and mortgages by mortgage holders, by region and age from the Living Costs and Food Survey for the
financial year ending 2022. Data is presented as a proportion of total expenditure and a proportion of disposable income.

8. Glossary

Disability status

To define disability in this publication, we refer to the Government Statistical Service (GSS) harmonised "core" definition of disability (https://analysisfunction.civilservice.gov.uk/policy-store/measuring-disability-for-the-equality-act-2010/): this identifies "disabled" as a person who has a physical or mental health condition or illness that has lasted or is expected to last 12 months or more that reduces their ability to carry-out day-to-day activities. The GSS harmonised questions are asked of the respondent in the survey, meaning that disability status is self-reported.

Ethnicity

The ethnicity disaggregation used has been chosen to provide the most granular breakdown possible, while producing robust estimates based on sample sizes, in line with harmonised standards for ethnicity data (https://analysisfunction.civilservice.gov.uk/policy-store/ethnicity-harmonised-standard/).

The five-category ethnicity breakdown includes:

- Asian or Asian British: Indian, Pakistani, Bangladeshi, Chinese or any other Asian background

- Black, African, Caribbean or Black British: African, Caribbean or Any other Black, African or Caribbean background

- Mixed and Multiple ethnic groups: White and Black Caribbean, White and Black African, White and Asian or Any other Mixed and Multiple ethnic background

- Other ethnic background group: Arab or Any other ethnic group

- White: White British, White Irish, Other White

Logistic regression

We carried out a logistic regression analysis to identify the individual characteristics associated with financial vulnerability. This further allows us to identify someone with a particular characteristic having higher or lower odds of experiencing some form of financial vulnerability when compared with a specified reference group, after taking other possible characteristics into account.

For example, if a particular group has an odds ratio of more than one, they are more likely than the reference group to be considered financially vulnerable when compared with the reference group.

Odds ratio

An odds ratio indicates the likelihood of experiencing some form of financial vulnerability given a particular characteristic. When a characteristic has an odds ratio of one, this means there is neither an increase nor a decrease in the likelihood of experiencing some form of financial vulnerability compared with the reference category. An odds ratio greater than one indicates an increased likelihood of experiencing some form of financial vulnerability compared with the reference category. An odds ratio less than one indicates a decreased likelihood of experiencing some form of financial vulnerability compared with the reference category.

Parental status

An adult is defined as a parent if they are the parent of a dependent child living in the household. Dependent children in this case includes children and stepchildren.

Parents were classified into two further groups; having a dependent child aged under 5 years or having a dependent child aged 5 years and over living in the household. Where parents have multiple dependent children in their household, they are included in a group based on the age of their youngest dependent child in their household.

A dependent child is someone aged under 16 years or someone who is aged 16 to 18 years, has never been married and is in full-time education.

Personal annual income

Personal annual gross income is self-reported on the Opinions and Lifestyle Survey (OPN) and therefore should be treated with caution.

A respondent's income information does not represent equivalised household income, that considers that households with more people will need a higher income to achieve the same standard of living as households with fewer members.

Those reporting no source of income may include those dependent on other members of their household, such as people aged 16 to 19 years who are in full-time education.

Income quintiles are calculated by ranking respondents from lowest to highest reported personal annual gross income and dividing them into five equal groups.

Those in the lowest quintile are those with a personal annual income below £11,230. Those in the lowest quintile could include those who have retired but still have other sources of income, in addition to those who are in employment but receiving a relatively low income.

Those in the highest quintile are those respondents with a personal annual income over £38,400.

Not all respondents provided information on their personal annual gross income, with some only able to provide a banded estimate or providing no information. These respondents are excluded from any analysis by income quintile.

Receiving support from charities

Receiving support from charities refers to a respondent self-reporting on the OPN "Using support from charities, including food banks" in response to the question "Which of these, if any, are you doing because of the increases in the cost of living? I am...".

Receiving benefits or financial support

Receiving benefits or financial support refers to a respondent self-reporting receiving income support, tax credits or universal credits, or other state benefits as one of their sources of income on the OPN. Those who reported receiving a state pension or child benefits only are not included in this category.

Statistical significance

This article presents a summary of results, with further data including confidence intervals (https://www.ons.gov.uk/methodology/methodologytopicsandstatisticalconcepts/uncertaintyandhowwemeasureit#confidence-interval) for the estimates shown in the charts presented contained in the associated datasets. Where comparisons between groups are presented, 95% confidence intervals should be used to assess the statistical significance (https://www.ons.gov.uk/methodology/methodologytopicsandstatisticalconcepts/uncertaintyandhowwemeasureit#statistical-significance) of the change.

For the regression analysis, characteristics were found to be significant based on the p-value associated (Wald Chi-Squared Test) with each characteristic. The odds ratios were then assessed alongside a confidence interval around each category of interest.

9. Data sources and quality

Quality

More quality and methodology information on the Opinions and Lifestyle Survey (OPN) and its strengths, limitations, appropriate uses, and how the data were created is available in our Opinions and Lifestyle Survey Quality and Methodology Information (https://www.ons.gov.uk/peoplepopulationandcommunity/healthandsocialcare/healthandlifeexpectancies/methodologies/opinionsandlifestylesurveyqmi).

Sampling

The analysis throughout this article is based on adults aged 16 years and over in Great Britain. The analysis in this report is based on 14,821 adults from a pooled dataset comprising six waves of data collection, covering the following periods:

- 8 to 19 February 2023
- 22 February to 5 March 2023
- 8 to 19 March 2023
- 22 March to 2 April 2023
- 5 to 16 April 2023
- 19 April to 1 May 2023

Further information on the survey design and quality can be found in our Opinions and Lifestyle Survey Quality and Methodology Information (https://www.ons.gov.uk/peoplepopulationandcommunity/healthandsocialcare/healthandlifeexpectancies/methodologies/opinionsandlifestylesurveyqmi).

Weighting

Survey weights were applied to make estimates representative of the population.

Weights were first adjusted for non-response and attrition. Subsequently, the weights were calibrated to satisfy population distributions considering the following factors: sex by age, region, tenure, highest qualification and employment status.

For age, sex and region, population totals based on projections of mid-year population estimates for June 2021 were used. The resulting weighted sample is therefore representative of the Great Britain adult population by a number of socio-demographic factors and geography.

Comparing over time

Changes were made to the survey methodology in the latest pooled period, 8 February to 1 May 2023; therefore, comparisons with previous pooled periods should be treated with caution.

Regression analysis

The analysis from the regression model presented in this article identifies differences between adults who were considered to be financially vulnerable (dependent variable), when compared with adults not considered to be financially vulnerable, while controlling for a range of characteristics (independent variables).

Three logistic regression models were produced to explain the relationships between the dependent and independent variables. These were:

- unadjusted: these models show the relationship between the dependent variable, and an independent variable of interest (characteristic)

- age and sex adjusted: these models looked at the same dependent and independent variables of interest while also controlling for age and sex

- fully adjusted: these models looked at the same dependent variable and a range of independent variables (characteristics) of interest while controlling for all variables

Missing values were excluded from the regression analysis where a response was not provided for a question or variable included in the model. As a result, 12,688 adults were included in the fully-adjusted regression model analysis.

The results of the modelling and a full breakdown of sample sizes and population estimates for each of the characteristics included in the fully adjusted regression model are available in the accompanying dataset (https://www.ons.gov.uk/peoplepopulationandcommunity/personalandhouseholdfinances/expenditure/datasets/impactofincreasedcostoflivingonadultsacrossgreatbritain).

Qualitative analysis

Between 19 April and 1 May 2023, survey respondents were asked; "Finally, in your own words, tell us about your experiences with the increases in cost of living." Latent Dirichlet Allocation (LDA) topic modelling (a Natural Language Processing method) was used on over 1900 responses.

A review of this by multiple experienced qualitative researchers, led to the agreement of a five-theme model:

- "Well-being and worries about the future"

- "Response by government and businesses"

- "Worry about others"

- "Shopping habits"

- "Widening inequality"

The qualitative researchers reviewed a total of 10 responses per theme. This was to label these themes and summarise the overall meaning of that theme using a range of supporting quotes from the respondents in the survey.

All survey responses were anonymous and any potentially identifying information has been removed from the quotes.

Acknowledgements

The qualitative analysis shown in this article was conducted by:

- Graham Brennan

- Priya Tanna

- Mercedesz Soos

New analysis from the Living Costs and Food Survey for the financial year ending 2022 was conducted by:

- Lee Colvin

- Paula Croal

10. Related links

Public opinions and social trends, Great Britain: 28 June to 9 July 2023

(https://www.ons.gov.uk/releases/publicopinionsandsocialtrendsgreatbritain28juneto9july2023)

Bulletin | Released 14 July 2023

Social insights on daily life and events, including the cost of living, working arrangements and well-being from the Opinions and Lifestyle Survey (OPN).

Impact of increased cost of living on adults across Great Britain: September 2022 to January 2023

(https://www.ons.gov.uk/peoplepopulationandcommunity/personalandhouseholdfinances/expenditure/articles/impactofincreasedcosto flivingonadultsacrossgreatbritain/september2022tojanuary2023)

Article | Released 20 February 2023

Analysis of the proportion of the population that are affected by an increase in their cost of living, and of the characteristics associated with having difficulty affording or being behind on energy, mortgage or rental payments, using data from the Opinions and Lifestyle Survey.

Family spending in the UK: April 2021 to March 2022

(https://www.ons.gov.uk/peoplepopulationandcommunity/personalandhouseholdfinances/expenditure/bulletins/familyspendingintheuk /april2021tomarch2022)

Bulletin | Released 31 May 2023

Average weekly household expenditure on goods and services in the UK, by age, income, economic status, socio-economic class, household composition and region.

Cost of living latest insights (https://www.ons.gov.uk/economy/inflationandpriceindices/articles/costofliving/latestinsights)

Insights tool | Updated daily

The latest data and trends about the cost of living. Explore changes in the cost of everyday items and how this is affecting people.

Tracking the impact of winter pressures in Great Britain: November 2022 to February 2023

(https://www.ons.gov.uk/peoplepopulationandcommunity/wellbeing/articles/trackingtheimpactofwinterpressuresingreatbritain/novemb er2022tofebruary2023)

Article | Released 24 April 2023

Insights from our Winter Survey as we tracked participants to examine how increases in the cost of living and difficulty accessing NHS services had impacted their lives during the winter months.

Characteristics of adults experiencing energy and food insecurity in Great Britain: 22 November to 18 December 2022

(https://www.ons.gov.uk/peoplepopulationandcommunity/wellbeing/articles/characteristicsofadultsexperiencingenergyandfoodinsecurit ygreatbritain/22novemberto18december2022)

Article | Released 13 February 2023

Understanding the characteristics associated with experiencing energy and food insecurity; logistic regression analysis using data from the Winter Survey.

The cost of living, current and upcoming work: February 2023

(https://www.ons.gov.uk/economy/inflationandpriceindices/articles/thecostoflivingcurrentandupcomingwork/february2023)

Article | Released 8 February 2023

A summary of our current and future analytical work related to the cost of living.

11. Cite this article

Office for National Statistics (ONS), released 14 July 2023, ONS website, article, <u>Impact of increased cost of living on adults across Great Britain: February to May 2023</u> (<u>https://www.ons.gov.uk/peoplepopulationandcommunity/personalandhouseholdfinances/expenditure/articles/impactofincreasedcostoflivingonadultsacrossgreatbritain/februarytomay2023</u>)

Contact details for this article

Lili Chowdhury, Caleb Ogwuru, Chris Jones, David Ainslie and Tim Vizard
policy.evidence.analysis@ons.gov.uk
Telephone: +44 300 0671543

Office for
National Statistics

Data and analysis from Census 2021

Cost of living and depression in adults, Great Britain: 29 September to 23 October 2022

Analysis into the prevalence of depression among adults in Great Britain in autumn 2022. Exploring this in the context of the rising cost of living.

Contact:
Cullum Attwell, Rachel Mullis, Bonang Lewis, Tim Vizard

Release date:
6 December 2022

Table of contents

1. Main points

The following information is for the period 29 September to 23 October 2022, based on adults in Great Britain.

- Around 1 in 6 (16%) adults experienced moderate to severe depressive symptoms; this is similar to rates found in summer 2021 (17%), however higher than pre-pandemic levels (10%).

- When comparing within population groups, prevalence of moderate to severe depressive symptoms was higher among adults who were economically inactive because of long-term sickness (59%), unpaid carers for 35 or more hours a week (37%), disabled adults (35%), adults in the most deprived areas of England (25%), young adults aged 16 to 29 years (28%) and women (19%).

- Around 1 in 4 (24%) of those who reported difficulty paying their energy bills experienced moderate to severe depressive symptoms, which is nearly three times higher than those who found it easy to pay their energy bills (9%).

- Around 1 in 4 (27%) adults who reported difficulty in affording their rent or mortgage payments had moderate to severe depressive symptoms; this is around two times higher compared with those who reported that it was easy (15%)

- Nearly a third (32%) of those experiencing moderate to severe depressive symptoms reported that they had to borrow more money or use more credit than usual in the last month compared with a year ago; this is higher compared with around 1 in 6 (18%) of those with no or mild depressive symptoms.

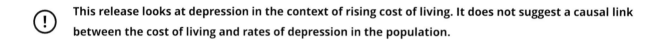 **This release looks at depression in the context of rising cost of living. It does not suggest a causal link between the cost of living and rates of depression in the population.**

2. Prevalence of moderate to severe depressive symptoms

The presence of some form of depression was indicated by a score of 10 or more on the eight-item Patient Health Questionnaire (PHQ8), which is also referred to as moderate to severe depressive symptoms. Further information can be found in the Glossary (https://www.ons.gov.uk/peoplepopulationandcommunity/healthandsocialcare/mentalhealth/articles/costoflivinganddepressioninadultsgreatbritain/29septemberto23october2022#glossary).

The estimates reported in this article are based on the period 29 September to 23 October 2022 ("autumn 2022").

In autumn 2022, around 1 in 6 (16%) adults aged 16 years and over reported moderate to severe depressive symptoms (Figure 1). This is similar to summer 2021 (17% over the period 21 July to 15 August 2021), a period before the rising of cost of living in Great Britain. Although there does not appear to be a change in the rate of depression following an increase in the cost of living, rates of depression remained higher than those seen before the coronavirus (COVID-19) pandemic (July 2019 to March 2020), where 10% of adults experienced some form of depression.

Figure 1: In autumn 2022, 1 in 6 (16%) adults aged 16 years and over reported moderate to severe depressive symptoms

Percentage of adults with moderate to severe depressive symptoms, Great Britain, July 2019 to October 2022

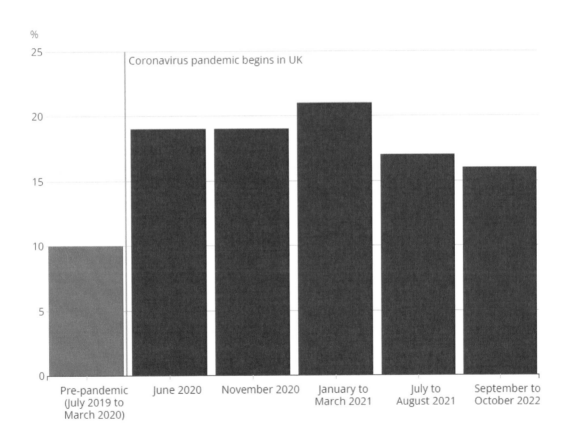

Source: Office for National Statistics – Opinions and Lifestyle Survey

Notes:

1. Base population: All adults aged 16 and over in Great Britain.

Download the data

.xlsx (https://www.ons.gov.uk/visualisations/dvc2370/fig1/datadownload.xlsx)

Previous estimates of adults experiencing some form of depression were published in August 2020 (https://www.ons.gov.uk/peoplepopulationandcommunity/wellbeing/articles/coronavirusanddepressioninadultsgreatbritain/june2020), December 2020 (https://www.ons.gov.uk/peoplepopulationandcommunity/healthandsocialcare/healthandwellbeing/bulletins/coronavirusandthesocialimpactsongreatbritain/11december2020#characteristics-of-adults-experiencing-some-form-of-depression-or-anxiety), May 2021 (https://www.ons.gov.uk/peoplepopulationandcommunity/wellbeing/articles/coronavirusanddepressioninadultsgreatbritain/januarytomarch2021) and October 2021 (https://www.ons.gov.uk/peoplepopulationandcommunity/wellbeing/articles/coronavirusanddepressioninadultsgreatbritain/latest).

Time series estimates of depressive symptoms by characteristics, including age, sex and region, can be found in the accompanying dataset (https://www.ons.gov.uk/peoplepopulationandcommunity/healthandsocialcare/mentalhealth/datasets/costoflivinganddepressioninadultsgreatbritain).

One of the services available to adults experiencing common mental disorders such as depression is talking therapies. Data from NHS Digital (Improving Access to Psychological Therapies (IAPT) (https://digital.nhs.uk/data-and-information/publications/statistical/psychological-therapies-report-on-the-use-of-iapt-services)), found in August 2022, around 145,000 people accessed these talking therapies, representing an increase of 5% when compared with August 2021. This follows a decrease during the coronavirus (COVID-19) pandemic in April 2020, when the number of new referrals to IAPT decreased by 57% (compared with April 2019). In August 2022, around 9 in 10 (88.6%) of referrals waited less than six weeks (https://digital.nhs.uk/data-and-information/publications/statistical/psychological-therapies-report-on-the-use-of-iapt-services/august-2022-final-including-a-report-on-the-iapt-employment-advisers-pilot/waiting-times) to access IAPT services.

For a definition of IAPT, see the Glossary (https://www.ons.gov.uk/peoplepopulationandcommunity/healthandsocialcare/mentalhealth/articles/costoflivinganddepressioninadultsgreatbritain/29septemberto23october2022#glossary).

3. Characteristics of adults with moderate to severe depressive symptoms in autumn 2022

In autumn 2022, prevalence of moderate to severe depressive symptoms was higher among the following groups of adults:

- economically inactive because of long-term sickness (59%)

- unpaid carers for 35 or more hours a week (37%)

- disabled adults (35%)

- those in the most deprived areas of England (25%)

- young adults aged 16 to 29 years (28%)

- single person household (21%)

- women (19%)

The groups identified here are similar to previous studies looking at depression. For example, ONS data in 2021 (https://www.ons.gov.uk/peoplepopulationandcommunity/wellbeing/articles/coronavirusanddepressioninadultsgreatbritain/julytoaugust2021) also found young adults and women, disabled adults, and adults in the most deprive areas were more likely to experience some form of depression. It is too early to say whether there has been a change in the groups of adults experiencing some form of depression, and it is something we will continue to explore.

 It is important to note that associations between characteristics and the presence of some form of depression may not reflect a causal relationship.

Figure 2: In autumn 2022, rates of some form of depression were higher amongst some population groups

Percentage of adults with moderate to severe depressive symptoms, Great Britain, 29 September to 23 October 2022

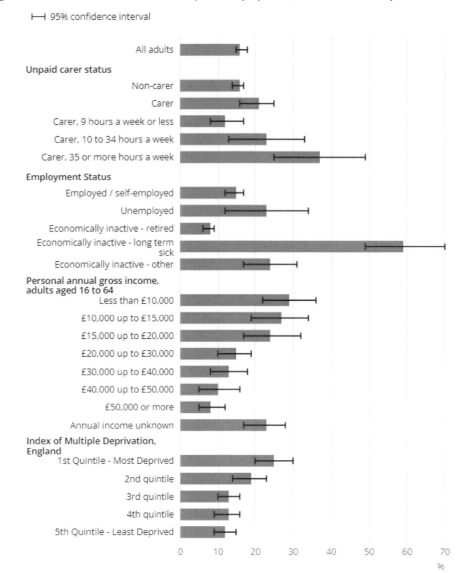

Source: Office for National Statistics (ONS) – Opinions and Lifestyle Survey (OPN)

Notes:

1. Base population: All adults aged 16 and over in Great Britain.

2. Further information on the definitions of population groups can be found in the accompanying dataset (https://www.ons.gov.uk/peoplepopulationandcommunity/healthandsocialcare/mentalhealth/datasets/costoflivinganddepressioninadultsgreatbritain).

Download the data

.xlsx (https://www.ons.gov.uk/visualisations/dvc2370/fig2/barchart/datadownload.xlsx)

Further information is available in the accompanying dataset (https://www.ons.gov.uk/peoplepopulationandcommunity/healthandsocialcare/mentalhealth/datasets/costoflivinganddepressioninadultsgreatbritain).

The reasons why the proportion of adults reporting some form of depression varies by individual characteristics are likely complex, as there are often associations between the individual characteristics considered.

Previous Office for National Statistics (ONS) regression analysis
(https://www.ons.gov.uk/peoplepopulationandcommunity/wellbeing/articles/coronavirusanddepressioninadultsgreatbritain/june2020)
controlling for a range of circumstances found younger adults, females, those living with a disability and those with lower incomes were
associated with moderate to severe depressive symptoms in the period 4 to 14 June 2020.

Other research shows that among adults with a probably Common Mental Disorder (CMD) (including depression), older age groups, males,
individuals reporting a disability and those of Asian ethnicity have been found to be underrepresented in Improving Access to Psychological
Therapies (IAPT) services. For further information see our Socio-demographic differences in use of Improving Access to Psychological
Therapies services, England: April 2017 to March 2018
(https://www.ons.gov.uk/peoplepopulationandcommunity/healthandsocialcare/mentalhealth/articles/sociodemographicdifferencesinuseoft
heimprovingaccesstopsychologicaltherapiesserviceengland/april2017tomarch2018).

Age and sex

In autumn 2022, adults aged 16 to 29 years were most likely to experience some form of depression (28%). People aged 70 years and over
were least likely to experience some form of depression (8%) when compared with any other age group.

Women were more likely (19%) than men (14%) to report experiencing some form of depression. This finding is consistent across all age
groups, in which women were more likely than men to experience some form of depression.

Over 1 in 3 (35%) women aged 16 to 29 years experienced moderate to severe depressive symptoms compared with 22% of men of the
same age (Figure 3). Prevalence of common mental health disorders including depression is also shown to be higher in women according to
the most recent Adult Psychiatric Morbidity Survey 2014 (PDF, 5.8MB)
(https://assets.publishing.service.gov.uk/government/uploads/system/uploads/attachment_data/file/556596/apms-2014-full-rpt.pdf).

Figure 3: Younger women were most likely to experience some form of depression

Percentage of adults with moderate to severe depressive symptoms, Great Britain, 29 September to 23 October 2022

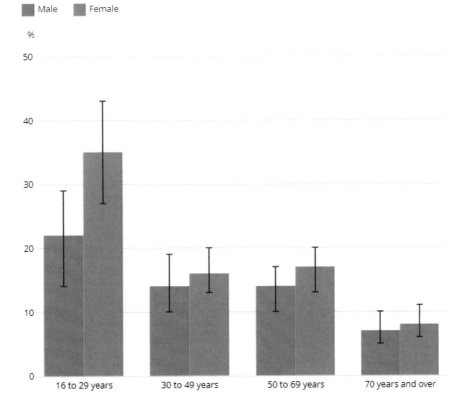

Source: Office for National Statistics (ONS) – Opinions and Lifestyle Survey (OPN)

Notes:

1. Base population: All adults aged 16 and over in Great Britain.

Download the data

.xlsx (https://www.ons.gov.uk/visualisations/dvc2370/fig3/datadownload.xlsx)

Disability and unpaid carer status

Disabled adults were five times (35%) more likely than non-disabled adults (7%) to experience some form of depression. Disabled adults may include those with a mental health condition or illness that has lasted or is expected to last 12 months or more. For a definition of disability, see the Glossary (https://www.ons.gov.uk/peoplepopulationandcommunity/healthandsocialcare/mentalhealth/articles/costoflivinganddepressioninadultsgreatbritain/29septemberto23october2022#glossary).

The proportion of adults with some form of depression was highest for unpaid carers who spent more than 35 hours a week caring (37%) compared with those who spent nine hours or less a week caring (12%) or with non-carers (16%).

For a definition of unpaid carers, see the Glossary (https://www.ons.gov.uk/peoplepopulationandcommunity/healthandsocialcare/mentalhealth/articles/costoflivinganddepressioninadultsgreatbritain/29septemberto23october2022#glossary).

Education and employment

Adults with below degree level qualifications were most likely to report moderate to severe depressive symptoms (19%) compared with those with a degree or equivalent qualification (12%). Of those with other qualifications, 15% experienced some form of depression.

The highest proportion of adults with moderate to severe depressive symptoms was those that were economically inactive because of long-term sickness (59%). Recent trends also show a 22% increase in inactivity in the labour market since 2019 (https://www.ons.gov.uk/employmentandlabourmarket/peoplenotinwork/economicinactivity/articles/halfamillionmorepeopleareoutofthelabourforcebecauseoflongtermsickness/2022-11-10), because of mental illness and nervous disorders.

Those who were economically inactive for other reasons (excluding being retired and long-term sickness) were more likely to experience some form of depression (24%) in autumn 2022 compared with those who were unemployed (23%) or those in employment (15%). Those who were retired (8%) were least likely to be experiencing some form of depression.

Being out of the labour market is known as "economic inactivity (https://www.ons.gov.uk/employmentandlabourmarket/peoplenotinwork/economicinactivity)" – this term refers to people who are not in work and have not been seeking or not been available for work.

Personal income

Among working age adults aged 16 to 64 years, those with lower gross personal annual incomes of less than £10,000 a year had the highest rates of moderate to severe depressive symptoms (29%) when compared with all higher income groups (Figure 2). The rates of moderate to severe depressive symptoms were lowest for those in the highest income group, 8% of those with a gross personal annual income of £50,000 or more.

Household characteristics

Adults living in single-person households were more likely to experience some form of depression (21%) compared with those in multi-person households (15%).

Of those with at least one child under the age of 16 years in the household, 17% reported moderate to severe depressive symptoms, a similar proportion to those living with no children under the age of 16 years in the household (16%).

Area deprivation

Adults living in the most deprived areas of England (based on the Index of Multiple Deprivation) were twice as likely to experience some form of depression in autumn 2022 (25%) than adults living in the least deprived areas (12%).

For further geographical breakdowns by region and country see our accompanying dataset (https://www.ons.gov.uk/peoplepopulationandcommunity/healthandsocialcare/mentalhealth/datasets/costoflivinganddepressioninadultsgreatbritain).

For a definition of area deprivation, see the Glossary (https://www.ons.gov.uk/peoplepopulationandcommunity/healthandsocialcare/mentalhealth/articles/costoflivinganddepressioninadultsgreatbritain/29septemberto23october2022#glossary).

4. Cost of living and depressive symptoms

This section explores differences in some form of depression (moderate to severe depressive symptoms) by a range of cost of living indicators.

 It is important to note that associations between cost of living indicators and the presence of some sort of depression may not reflect a causal relationship.

Depressive symptoms and energy costs

Among adults who pay energy bills, around 2 in 5 (43%) reported they found it very or somewhat difficult to afford them. Around half (47%) reported they found it very or somewhat easy to pay their energy bills.

Around 1 in 4 (24%) of those who reported it was very or somewhat difficult to pay their energy bills experienced some form of depression. This is nearly three times higher than those who found it very or somewhat easy to pay their energy bills (9%).

For further analysis on the characteristics associated with having difficulty affording energy bills, see our Impact of increased cost of living on adults across Great Britain: June to September 2022 (https://www.ons.gov.uk/peoplepopulationandcommunity/personalandhouseholdfinances/expenditure/articles/impactofincreasedcostoflivin gonadultsacrossgreatbritain/junetoseptember2022#characteristics-of-adults-who-are-experiencing-difficulty-or-are-behind-with-energy-rent-or-mortgage-payments).

Depressive symptoms and tenure

Among those who own their property outright, around 1 in 10 (10%) experienced some form of depression. This rose to around 1 in 8 (13%) among those that are currently paying off a mortgage and/or loan that helped to purchase the property and increased further to around 1 in 4 (27%) among those that are renting.

Research of Understanding Society data found renters were more likely to report higher levels of distress than homeowners (https://www.jrf.org.uk/report/anxiety-nation-economic-insecurity-and-mental-distress-2020s-britain), based on 12 markers of mental health problems.

Depressive symptoms and housing costs

Among adults currently making rent or mortgage payments, around a third (33%) reported an increase in these payments in the past six months, and around half (54%) did not report an increase.

Among adults who reported an increase in rent or mortgage payments in the last six months, around 1 in 5 (22%) experienced some form of depression. This is higher compared with those who did not report an increase in rent or mortgage payments in the last six months (16%).

Among adults currently making rent or mortgage payments, around 1 in 3 (32%) reported they found it very or somewhat difficult to afford them. Around half (51%) of adults making rent or mortgage payments reported they found it very or somewhat easy to afford these payments.

Around 1 in 4 (27%) adults who reported that it was very or somewhat difficult to afford their rent/mortgage payments had some form of depression; this is higher compared with around 1 in 7 (15%) who reported that it was very or somewhat easy.

Research published in July 2017 showed around 1 in 5 (23%) English adults said that a housing issue had negatively impacted upon their mental health (https://england.shelter.org.uk/professional_resources/policy_and_research/policy_library/research_the_impact_of_housing_problems_on_m ental_health) in the last five years.

For further analysis on the characteristics associated with having difficulty affording mortgage or rent payments, see our Impact of increased cost of living on adults across Great Britain: June to September 2022 (https://www.ons.gov.uk/peoplepopulationandcommunity/personalandhouseholdfinances/expenditure/articles/impactofincreasedcostoflivingonadultsacrossgreatbritain/junetoseptember2022#characteristics-of-adults-who-are-experiencing-difficulty-or-are-behind-with-energy-rent-or-mortgage-payments).

5. Worries and perceptions of adults with depression

The analysis reported in this section explores the worries and perceptions of issues facing the UK, comparing responses of those with some form of depression (moderate to severe depressive symptoms) to those with no or mild depressive symptoms. Further information can be found in the Glossary (https://www.ons.gov.uk/peoplepopulationandcommunity/healthandsocialcare/mentalhealth/articles/costoflivinganddepressioninadultsgreatbritain/29septemberto23october2022#glossary).

Worries

Around 9 in 10 (92%) adults with some form of depression reported being very or somewhat worried about the rising cost of living (Figure 4); this is higher compared with three-quarters (75%) of adults with no or mild depressive symptoms.

Figure 4: Adults with moderate to severe depressive symptoms were more worried about the rising cost of living

Proportion of adults by depressive symptoms in Great Britain who are very or somewhat worried, 29 September to 23 October 2022

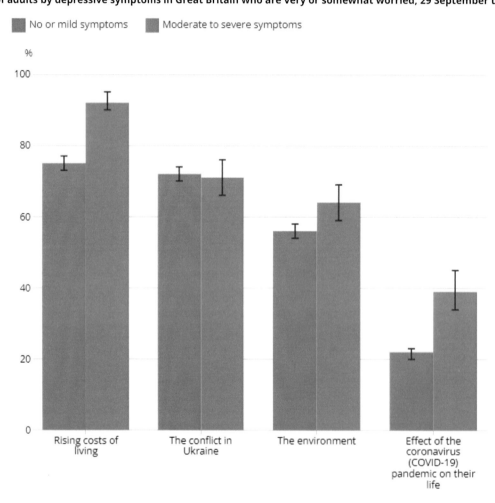

Source: Office for National Statistics (ONS) – Opinions and Lifestyle Survey (OPN)

Notes:

1. Questions: "In the past two weeks, how worried or unworried have you been about rising costs of living?", "In the past two weeks, how worried or unworried have you been about the environment?", "In the past two weeks, how worried or unworried have you been about the conflict in Ukraine?" and "How worried or unworried are you about the effect that the coronavirus (COVID-19) pandemic is having on your life right now?".

2. Base: All adults aged 16 and over in Great Britain with moderate to severe and no or mild depressive symptoms.

Download the data

.xlsx (https://www.ons.gov.uk/visualisations/dvc2370/fig4/datadownload.xlsx)

Issues

When asked about the important issues facing the UK today, 97% of adults with some form of depression reported the cost of living (Figure 5). This is slightly higher compared with those with no or mild depressive symptoms (93%).

The biggest differences in issues reported by adults with some form of depression compared with those with no or mild symptoms were:

- housing: 62% compared with 46%
- employment: 46% compared with 32%
- education: 45% compared with 37%

Figure 5: Among adults with moderate to severe depressive symptoms, 97% reported cost of living as an issue

Proportion of adults by depressive symptoms in Great Britain, 29 September to 23 October 2022

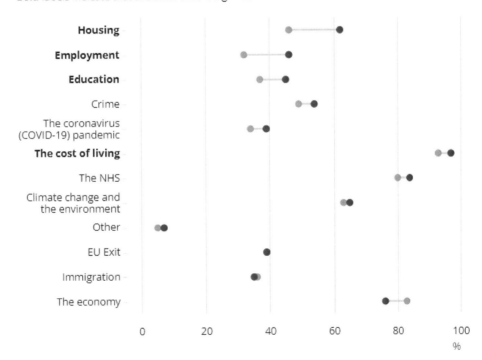

Source: Office for National Statistics (ONS) – Opinions and Lifestyle Survey (OPN)

Notes:

1. Question: "What do you think are important issues facing the UK today?". Please note that no additional context was provided around the question or response options on the survey.

2. Base: All adults aged 16 and over in Great Britain with moderate to severe and no or mild depressive symptoms.

3. Respondents were able to choose more than one option.

4. The percentage of adults who reported "None of these" have not been included in the chart because respondents who selected this response option were unable to select any other response option.

Download the data

.xlsx (https://www.ons.gov.uk/visualisations/dvc2370/fig5/datadownload.xlsx)

6. Responses to cost of living

This section explores experiences and responses to the rising cost of living, comparing adults with moderate to severe and no to mild depressive symptoms.

 It is important to note that associations between cost of living indicators and the presence of some form of depression may not reflect a causal relationship.

Responses to changes in the cost of living

In autumn 2022, adults were asked about their actions in response to the rising cost of living (Figure 6).

When asked about their actions in response to increases in the cost of living, 59% of those with moderate to severe depressive symptoms reported spending less on food shopping and essentials. This was nearly two times lower compared with those with no or mild depressive symptoms (35%). Adults with moderate to severe depressive symptoms were also more likely (73%) to spend less on non-essentials compared with those with no or mild depressive symptoms (64%).

Around 1 in 16 (6%) adults with moderate to severe depressive symptoms reported using support from charities, including food banks. This is higher compared with 1% of adults with no or mild depressive symptoms.

Figure 6: Around a quarter (24%) of adults with moderate to severe depressive symptoms reported using credit more than usual

Proportion of adults by depressive symptoms in Great Britain, 29 September to 23 October 2022

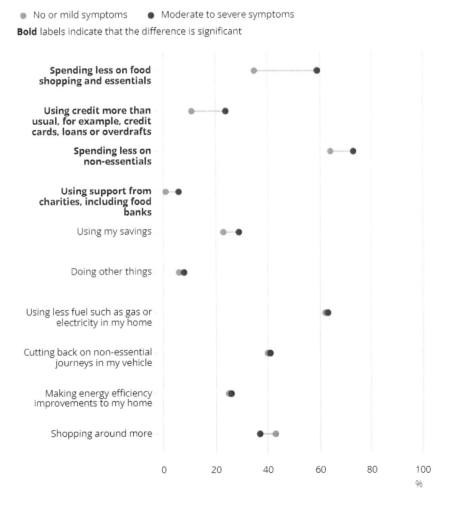

Source: Office for National Statistics (ONS) – Opinions and Lifestyle Survey (OPN)

Notes:

1. Question: "Which of these, if any, are you doing because of the increases in the cost of living?".

2. Base: All adults aged 16 and over in Great Britain with moderate to severe and no or mild depressive symptoms.

3. Respondents were able to choose more than one option.

4. The wording for some response options have been shortened. See the accompanying dataset for full response options presented on survey.

5. The percentage of adults who reported "None of these" have not been included in the chart because respondents who selected this response option were unable to select any other response option. See accompanying dataset (https://www.ons.gov.uk/peoplepopulationandcommunity/healthandsocialcare/mentalhealth/datasets/costoflivinganddepressioninadultsgreatbritain).

Download the data

.xlsx (https://www.ons.gov.uk/visualisations/dvc2370/fig6/datadownload.xlsx)

Borrowing and savings

Research has found that during the pandemic financial hardship was more likely to affect those with mental health problems (https://mmhpistage.wpengine.com/publications/the-state-were-in/).

For those experiencing some form of depression, 24% of adults said they were using credit more than usual (for example, credit cards, loans or overdrafts). This was in comparison with 11% with no or mild depressive symptoms (Figure 6).

Nearly a third (32%) of adults experiencing moderate to severe depressive symptoms in autumn 2022 reported that they had to borrow more money or use more credit than usual in the last month compared with a year ago. This compared with 18% of those with no or mild depressive symptoms.

Among adults with moderate to severe depressive symptoms, around 1 in 5 (21%) reported that they expect to be able to save some money over the next 12 months; this was lower compared with around 2 in 5 (38%) of adults with no or mild depressive symptoms.

Financial situations

Adults were asked if their household could afford an unexpected, but necessary expense of £850. This gives us an indication of who may be struggling financially.

Focusing on the financial characteristics of those with moderate to severe depressive symptoms, over half (52%) reported being unable to afford an unexpected expense of £850. This was higher compared with around a quarter (26%) of adults with no or mild depressive symptoms.

Impacts of cost of living on work

Around 2 in 5 working adults (43%) with moderate to severe depressive symptoms reported making no changes at work because of the cost of living increases compared with around 3 in 5 (61%) working adults reporting no or mild depressive symptoms.

Around a third (34%) of working adults with some form of depression reported looking for a job that pays more money (including a promotion) (Figure 7). This is higher compared with 17% of working adults with no or mild depressive symptoms.

Almost one-quarter (22%) of working adults experiencing some form of depression reported that they were working more hours than usual in their main job, compared with around 1 in 6 (16%) working adults who experienced no or mild depressive symptoms.

Figure 7: Around a third (34%) of working adults with moderate to severe depressive symptoms are looking for a job that pays more money, including a promotion

Proportion of adults by depressive symptoms in Great Britain, 29 September to 23 October 2022

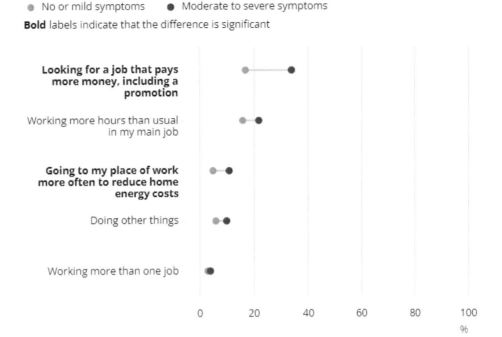

Source: Office for National Statistics (ONS) – Opinions and Lifestyle Survey (OPN)

Notes:

1. Question: "Thinking of your work situation, which of these, if any, are you doing because of the increases in the cost of living?".

2. Base: Working adults aged 16 and over in Great Britain with moderate to severe and no or mild depressive symptoms.

3. Respondents were able to choose more than one option.

4. The percentage of adults who reported "None of these" have not been included in the chart because respondents who selected this response option were unable to select any other response option.

Download the data

.xlsx (https://www.ons.gov.uk/visualisations/dvc2370/fig7/datadownload.xlsx)

The reasons why there is a higher proportion of adults with some form of depression making changes to their work situation in response to increases in the cost of living are likely complex. Consideration is needed for the associations between characteristics as well as the individuals' work circumstances.

This could partly be explained by age, given that a higher percentage of young adults experienced moderate to severe depressive symptoms (Section 3 (https://www.ons.gov.uk/peoplepopulationandcommunity/healthandsocialcare/mentalhealth/articles/costoflivinganddepressioninadultsgreatbritain/29septemberto23october2022#characteristics-of-adults-with-moderate-to-severe-depressive-symptoms-in-autumn-2022)). Furthermore, according to analysis published in our Public opinions and social trends release (https://www.ons.gov.uk/peoplepopulationandcommunity/wellbeing/datasets/publicopinionsandsocialtrendsgreatbritainhouseholdfinances), younger people are also more likely to be making changes to their work situation in response to the cost of living.

7. Cost of living and depression data

Cost of living and depression in adults, Great Britain
(https://www.ons.gov.uk/peoplepopulationandcommunity/healthandsocialcare/mentalhealth/datasets/costoflivinganddepressioninadult
sgreatbritain)

Dataset | Released 6 December 2022

Analysis of the proportion of the British adult population experiencing some form of depression in autumn 2022, including experiences of changes in cost of living and household finances. Analysis based on the Opinions and Lifestyle Survey.

8. Glossary

Area deprivation, England

Area deprivation is measured using the Index of Multiple Deprivation (IMD) (https://www.gov.uk/government/statistics/english-indices-of-deprivation-2019). This is the official measure of relative deprivation for small areas in England. The IMD ranks every small area in England from 1 (most deprived area) to 32,844 (least deprived area). We have grouped areas into five groups (quintiles), ranging from most deprived to least deprived areas.

Depressive symptoms

The presence of some form of depression was indicated by a score of 10 or more on the eight-item Patient Health Questionnaire (PHQ8), which is also referred to as moderate to severe depressive symptoms. A score of less than 10 indicated a lack of some form of depression, which is also referred to as no more mild depressive symptoms.

Respondents were asked the following questions from the eight-item Patient Health Questionnaire (PHQ-8) (https://www.phqscreeners.com/):

a. Over the last two weeks, how often have you been bothered by having little interest or pleasure in doing things?

b. Over the last two weeks, how often have you been bothered by feeling down, depressed or hopeless?

c. Over the last two weeks, how often have you been bothered by having trouble falling or staying asleep, or sleeping too much?

d. Over the last two weeks, how often have you been bothered by feeling tired or having little energy?

e. Over the last two weeks, how often have you been bothered by having a poor appetite or overeating?

f. Over the last two weeks, how often have you been bothered by feeling negative about yourself or that you are a failure or have let yourself or your family down?

g. Over the last two weeks, how often have you been bothered by having trouble concentrating on things, such as reading the newspaper or watching television?

h. Over the last two weeks, how often have you been bothered by moving or speaking so slowly that other people could have noticed; or being so fidgety or restless that you have been moving around a lot more than usual?

These questions had four response options ranging from 0 (Not at all) to 3 (Nearly every day). A "depression score" was then derived by summing all responses chosen, resulting in a score ranging from 0 to 24. The higher the score, the greater the severity of depressive symptoms.

A person's PHQ-8 score sits in one of two categories:

- no or mild depressive symptoms – this refers to a depression (PHQ-8) score of between 0 and 9 (inclusive)
- moderate to severe depressive symptoms – this refers to a depression (PHQ-8) score of between 10 and 24 (inclusive)

Disability status

To define disability in this publication, we refer to the Government Statistical Service (GSS) harmonised "core" definition (https://analysisfunction.civilservice.gov.uk/policy-store/measuring-disability-for-the-equality-act-2010/). This identifies "disabled" as a person who has a physical or mental health condition or illness that has lasted or is expected to last 12 months or more and that reduces their ability to carry-out day-to-day activities. As such, this group will include those with mental health conditions such as depression. The GSS harmonised questions are asked of the respondent in the survey, meaning that disability status is self-reported.

Improving Access to Psychological Therapies (IAPT) services

Improving Access to Psychological Therapies (IAPT) services is an NHS service designed to offer psychological talking therapies to adults living in England who experience common mental health problems such as stress, anxiety disorders and depression. Patients need to be registered with a GP in England to access the services, but they do not need referral from the GP to access it. IAPT services offers a variety of different treatments (https://www.nhs.uk/mental-health/talking-therapies-medicine-treatments/talking-therapies-and-counselling/types-of-talking-therapies/) such as guided self-help, Cognitive Behavioural Therapy (CBT), counselling, Interpersonal Therapy (IPT), mindfulness and many more. More information on IAPT services (https://digital.nhs.uk/data-and-information/publications/statistical/psychological-therapies-report-on-the-use-of-iapt-services) can be found on the NHS website.

Statistical significance

This report presents a summary of results, with further data including confidence intervals for the estimates contained in the accompanying dataset (https://www.ons.gov.uk/peoplepopulationandcommunity/healthandsocialcare/mentalhealth/datasets/costoflivinganddepressioninadultsgreatbritain). Where comparisons between groups are presented, 95% confidence intervals should be used to assess the statistical significance (https://www.ons.gov.uk/methodology/methodologytopicsandstatisticalconcepts/uncertaintyandhowwemeasureit#statistical-significance) of the differences.

Unpaid carers

Unpaid carer is defined using the Government Statistical Service (GSS) harmonised "core" definition: identifying an unpaid carer if they provide support or care to an individual who has needs because of physical or mental health condition(s) or illness(es), or problems related to old age. Unpaid carers status is self-reported.

A non-carer is defined as someone who answered "no" to the following question:

"Do you look after, or give any help or support to, anyone because they have long-term physical or mental health conditions or illnesses, or problems related to old age? Exclude anything you do as part of your paid employment."

9. Data sources and quality

Opinions and Lifestyle Survey

This release contains data and indicators from the Office for National Statistics (ONS) Opinions and Lifestyle Survey, which collects data from individuals (aged 16 years or older) in Great Britain.

Quality

More quality and methodology information on the Opinions and Lifestyle Survey (OPN) and its strengths, limitations, appropriate uses, and how the data were created is available in our Opinions and Lifestyle Survey Quality and Methodology Information (https://www.ons.gov.uk/peoplepopulationandcommunity/healthandsocialcare/healthandlifeexpectancies/methodologies/opinionsandlifestylesurveyqmi).

Sampling

The analysis throughout this report is based on adults aged 16 years and over in Great Britain with a valid depression score. The latest analysis in this report is based on 4,266 adults from a pooled dataset comprising two waves of data collection, covering the following periods:

- 29 September to 9 October 2022
- 12 to 23 October 2022

Pooling two waves of data together increases sample sizes, allowing us to explore depressive symptoms for different groups of the population.

Some questions refer in the "past 2 weeks" or the "past month". This refers to the period before when the question was asked to the respondent and may cover different time periods based on which survey wave they responded to.

Earlier periods referenced in Section 2 cover the following periods

- July 2019 to March 2020
- 4 to 14 June 2020
- 11 to 29 November 2020
- 27 January to 7 March 2021
- 21 July to 15 August 2021
- 29 September to 23 October 2022

Changes in estimates over time could be attributed to seasonality effects. However, seasonality effects have not been adjusted for in this analysis.

Weighting

Survey weights were applied to make estimates representative of the population.

Weights were adjusted for non-response. Subsequently, the weights were calibrated considering the following factors: sex by age, region, tenure, education and employment status.

For age, sex and region, population totals based on projections of mid-year population estimates for June 2021 were used. The resulting weighted sample is therefore representative of the Great Britain adult population by a number of socio-demographic factors and geography.

10. Strengths and limitations

The main strengths of this analysis include:

- the use of the Patient Health Questionnaire (PHQ-8) (https://www.phqscreeners.com/) provides a robust measure of the presence of some form of depression in the population

- robust methods are adopted for the survey's sampling and weighting strategies to limit the impact of bias

- quality assurance procedures are undertaken throughout the analysis stages to minimise the risk of error

The main limitations of this analysis include:

- the sample sizes for some groups of the population are relatively small, which means that confidence intervals around some estimates are larger, providing less certainty around the estimate; consequently, detailed analyses for some sub-groups are not possible

- data collected before the pandemic (July 2019 to March 2020) were achieved via a telephone interview, while data collected since the pandemic were predominantly online, with an option for telephone interview where online data collection was not possible; this means mode of data collection may have had an effect on the response given by adults to the survey questions when comparing data with this earlier period

11. Related links

Impact of increased cost of living on adults across Great Britain: June to September 2022
(https://www.ons.gov.uk/peoplepopulationandcommunity/personalandhouseholdfinances/expenditure/articles/impactofincreasedcosto
flivingonadultsacrossgreatbritain/junetoseptember2022)

Article | Released 25 October 2022

Analysis of the proportion of the population affected by an increase in their cost of living and the individual characteristics associated
with not being able to afford an unexpected expense, using data from the Opinions and Lifestyle Survey (OPN).

Worries about the rising costs of living, Great Britain: April to May 2022
(https://www.ons.gov.uk/peoplepopulationandcommunity/wellbeing/articles/worriesabouttherisingcostsoflivinggreatbritain/apriltomay2
022)

Article | Released 10 June 2022

An article covering people's worries about the rising costs of living, using data from the Opinions and Lifestyle Survey collected between
27 April and 22 May 2022 and based on adults in Great Britain aged 16 years and over.

Individual and community well-being, Great Britain: October 2022
(https://www.ons.gov.uk/peoplepopulationandcommunity/wellbeing/bulletins/individualandcommunitywellbeinggreatbritain/october20
22)

Article | Released 6 December 2022

Research into what matters for individual and community well-being in Great Britain. This has not been explored in a qualitative way by
the ONS since the Measures of National Well-being public debate in 2010. These data come from our Opinions and Lifestyle Survey.

Socio-demographic differences in use of Improving Access to Psychological Therapies services, England: April 2017 to March 2018
(https://www.ons.gov.uk/peoplepopulationandcommunity/healthandsocialcare/mentalhealth/articles/sociodemographicdifferencesinus
eoftheimprovingaccesstopsychologicaltherapiesserviceengland/april2017tomarch2018)

Bulletin | Released 17 June 2022

Characteristics of patients treated in the Improving Access to Psychological Therapies (IAPT) services and whether patients are
representative of the population with a probable Common Mental Disorder (CMD) as defined by the UK Household Longitudinal Study
(UKHLS) in England. This identifies groups with lower access to IAPT to help to improve the coverage of the service.

Economic inactivity due to long-term sickness, UK: 2019 to 2022
(https://www.ons.gov.uk/employmentandlabourmarket/peoplenotinwork/economicinactivity/articles/halfamillionmorepeopleareoutofth
elabourforcebecauseoflongtermsickness/2022-11-10)

Article | 10 November 2022

Between June and August 2022, around 2.5 million people reported long-term sickness as the main reason for economic inactivity, up
from around 2 million in 2019.

Coronavirus and depression in adults, Great Britain: July to August 2021
(https://www.ons.gov.uk/peoplepopulationandcommunity/wellbeing/articles/coronavirusanddepressioninadultsgreatbritain/julytoaugus
t2021)

Bulletin | Released 1 October 2021

Analysis of the proportion of the adult population of Great Britain experiencing some form of depression in summer 2021, based on the
Opinions and Lifestyle Survey. Includes analysis by age, sex and other characteristics and comparisons with early 2021, 2020 and pre-
pandemic estimates.

Coronavirus and the social impacts on Great Britain
(https://www.ons.gov.uk/peoplepopulationandcommunity/healthandsocialcare/healthandwellbeing/bulletins/coronavirusandthesociali
mpactsongreatbritain/11december2020#characteristics-of-adults-experiencing-some-form-of-depression-or-anxiety)

Bulletin | Released 11 December 2020

Indicators from the Opinions and Lifestyle Survey (covering 11 to 29 November 2020) of the impact of the coronavirus (COVID-19) pandemic on people, households and communities in Great Britain.

Coronavirus (COVID-19) in charts: What we learned over the past month (https://www.ons.gov.uk/peoplepopulationandcommunity/healthandsocialcare/conditionsanddiseases/articles/coronaviruscovid19inchartswhatwelearnedoverthepastmonth/2021-03-01)

Article | Released 1 March 2021

Data from across the UK government and devolved administrations highlight the effects of the pandemic on society and the economy.

Public opinions and social trends, Great Britain (https://www.ons.gov.uk/peoplepopulationandcommunity/wellbeing/bulletins/publicopinionsandsocialtrendsgreatbritain/8to20november2022)

Bulletin | Released on 25 November 2022

Social insights on daily life and events, including the cost of living, location of work, health and well-being from the Opinions and Lifestyle Survey (OPN).

12. Cite this article

Office for National Statistics (ONS), released 6 December 2022, ONS website, article, Cost of living and depression in adults, Great Britain: 29 September to 23 October 2022 (https://www.ons.gov.uk/peoplepopulationandcommunity/healthandsocialcare/mentalhealth/articles/costoflivinganddepressioninadultsgreatbritain/29septemberto23october2022)

Contact details for this article

Cullum Attwell, Rachel Mullis, Bonang Lewis, Tim Vizard
policy.evidence.analysis@ons.gov.uk
Telephone: +44 3000 671543

You might also be interested in:

Cost of living latest insights

Office for
National Statistics

Disability, England and Wales: Census 2021

Information on disability in England and Wales, Census 2021 data.

Contact:
Beth Waddington

Release date:
19 January 2023

Next release:
To be announced

Table of contents

1. Main points

This page is also available in <u>Welsh (Cymraeg) (PDF, 371KB) (https://static.ons.gov.uk/files/disability-england-and-wales-census-2021-welsh-full-bulletin.pdf)</u>.

- Age-standardised proportions (ASPs) are used throughout this bulletin, with the exception of the data on the number of disabled people within a household; ASPs allow for comparison between populations over time and across geographies, as they account for differences in the population size and age structure.

- In England, in 2021, a smaller proportion but larger number of people were disabled (17.7%, 9.8 million), compared with 2011 (19.3%, 9.4 million).

- In Wales, in 2021, a smaller proportion and a smaller number of people were disabled (21.1%, 670,000), compared with 2011 (23.4%, 696,000).

- The English region with the highest proportion of disabled people was the North East (21.2%, 567,000).

- Out of all local authorities across England and Wales, Blackpool (24.7%), Blaenau Gwent (24.6%) and Neath Port Talbot (24.6%) had the highest proportions of disabled people.

Tell us what you think about this publication by <u>answering a few questions (https://www.surveymonkey.co.uk/r/VPZFYG5)</u>.

2. Disability, England and Wales

Disability

To identify disability in England and Wales, we asked people "Do you have any physical or mental health conditions or illnesses lasting or expected to last 12 months or more?". If they answered yes, a further question "Do any of your conditions or illnesses reduce your ability to carry out day-to-day activities?" was presented. The identification of disability differs from the 2011 Census question used, which asked "Are your day-to-day activities limited because of a health problem or disability which has lasted, or expected to last, at least 12 months?".

The question changed in order to collect data that more closely aligned with the definition of disability in the Equality Act (2010 (https://www.gov.uk/guidance/equality-act-2010-guidance)). The Equality Act defines an individual as disabled if they have a physical or mental impairment that has a substantial and long-term negative effect on their ability to carry out normal day-to-day activities. The way we identify disabled people has therefore changed between 2011 and 2021 and this may have had an impact on the number of people identified as disabled. See Section 8: Measuring the data (https://www.ons.gov.uk/peoplepopulationandcommunity/healthandsocialcare/healthandwellbeing/bulletins/disabilityenglandandwales/census2021#measuring-the-data) for more information on the question change.

Census 2021 was undertaken during the coronavirus (COVID-19) pandemic, which may also have influenced how people perceive their health status and activity limitations and therefore may affect how people chose to respond.

Percentages in this bulletin have been age-standardised. Disability and age are closely related, with older people being more likely to be disabled. Age-standardised proportions (ASPs) account for different age structures in populations and are more appropriate than crude percentages when drawing comparisons over time and across areas. The numbers being reported here are the actual number who responded in each category. You can download both age-standardised and non-age standardised datasets (https://www.ons.gov.uk/peoplepopulationandcommunity/healthandsocialcare/healthandwellbeing/bulletins/disabilityenglandandwales/census2021#disability-england-and-wales-data). Read more in our blog Age-standardising data: What does this mean and why does it matter? (https://blog.ons.gov.uk/2023/01/19/age-standardising-data-what-does-this-mean-and-why-does-it-matter/)

Disability in England and Wales

In 2021, across both England and Wales, the proportion of disabled people was 17.8% (10.4 million). The proportion of people that are disabled has decreased 1.7 percentage points from 2011, when it was 19.5% (10.0 million).

Figure 1: Age-standardised disability, 2011 and 2021, England and Wales

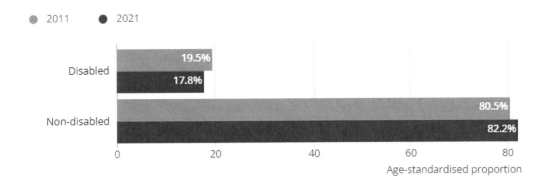

Source: Office for National Statistics – Census 2021

Download the data

.xlsx (https://www.ons.gov.uk/visualisations/dvc2218/disability_fig1/region_groupedbar/datadownload.xlsx)

3. How disability varied across England and Wales

Disability in England

In England, the proportion of disabled people decreased between censuses (from 19.3% in 2011 to 17.7% in 2021). However, there was an increase in the number of disabled people (from 9.4 million in 2011 to 9.8 million in 2021).

The proportion of disabled people decreased in every region of England. The region with the highest proportion of disabled people was the North East (21.2%, 567,000), as it had been in 2011 (22.8%, 562,000). In 2021, the North East was followed by the North West (19.8%, 1.4 million) and Yorkshire and The Humber (18.9%, 1.0 million). Meanwhile, London (15.7%, 1.2 million) and the South East (16.1%, 1.5 million) had the lowest proportions of disabled people.

The local authorities with the highest proportions of disabled people in 2021 included Blackpool (24.7%), at 7.0 percentage points above the national estimate for England, and Liverpool (23.8%), at 6.1 percentage points above the national estimate. Conversely, the local authorities with the lowest proportions of disabled people were the City of London (11.8%) and Elmbridge (12.2%).

Although the South East had a relatively low proportion of disabled people, the top four local authorities which had the largest increases in the proportion of disabled people, compared with 2011, were all in the South East. Namely, Gosport (20.0%), Eastbourne (20.3%), Lewes (18.8%) and the Isle of Wight (21.3%). These ranged from an increase of 1.1 to 1.4 percentage points.

The top five local authorities which had the largest decrease in the proportion of disabled people, compared with 2011, were all in London. Namely, Newham (17.5%), Tower Hamlets (20.1%), Brent (14.7%), Hackney (19.2%) and Barking and Dagenham (17.9%). These ranged from a decrease of 5.2 to 7.2 percentage points.

Disability in Wales

As in England, the proportion of the population in Wales who were disabled decreased in 2021 (21.1%, 670,000) compared with 2011 (23.4%, 696,000).

In Wales, the local authorities with the highest proportions of disabled people were Neath Port Talbot (24.6%), Blaenau Gwent (24.6%), and Merthyr Tydfil (24.2%).

In 2011, the same three local authorities had the highest proportions of disabled people in Wales: Merthyr Tydfil (28.8%), Blaenau Gwent (28.4%), and Neath Port Talbot (28.2%). This was higher than any local authority in England in 2011. In each of the three, the proportion of disabled people fell from 2011 to 2021.

Some of the local authorities in Wales with larger proportions of people reporting a disability are also areas in which larger proportions of people provided unpaid care. For more information, please see our Unpaid care, England and Wales: 2021 statistical bulletin (https://www.ons.gov.uk/peoplepopulationandcommunity/healthandsocialcare/healthandwellbeing/bulletins/unpaidcareenglandandwales/census2021).

The local authorities with the lowest proportion of disabled people were Monmouthshire (17.7%), Gwynedd (18.1%), and Powys (18.1%).

All local authorities in Wales saw a decrease in the proportion of people reporting a disability in 2021. The top four local authorities which had the largest decrease in the proportion of disabled people, compared with 2011, were Merthyr Tydfil (24.2%), Blaenau Gwent (24.6%), Caerphilly (23.6%), and Rhondda Cynon Taf (23.8%).

Figure 2: How disability (age-standardised) varied across local authorities in England and Wales, 2021

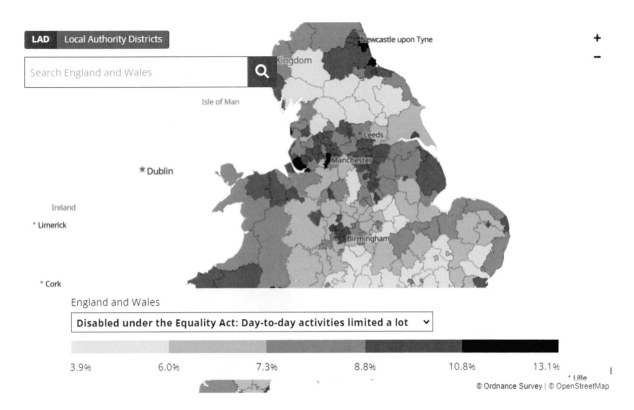

Note: This is a snapshot of an interactive image, to view the full image please go to: https://www.ons.gov.uk/peoplepopulationandcommunity/healthandsocialcare/healthandwellbeing/bulletins/disabilityenglandandwales/census2021

Source: Office for National Statistics – Census 2021

Download the data

.xlsx (https://www.ons.gov.uk/visualisations/dvc2218/disability_fig2/datadownload.xlsx)

4. The number of households where at least one person was identified as disabled

There were 24.8 million households across England and Wales in 2021, up 6.1% from 23.4 million in 2011.

We collected information on the number of household members that were disabled. It is not possible to age standardise at a household level, therefore, the proportions reported in this section are not standardised.

In England, the census data on disability within households show that:

- in 68.0% (15.9 million) of households, no people are disabled

- 25.4% (6.0 million) of households include one disabled member

- in the remaining 6.6% (1.6 million) of households, two or more people are disabled within the household

Households with two or more disabled people ranged from 5.1% (175,000) in London to 7.8% (92,000) in the North East.

The English local authorities with the highest proportion of two or more disabled people within a household were East Lindsey (10.3%), Bolsover (9.6%), and Knowsley (9.5%).

In Wales, the census data on disability within households show that:

- in 62.1% (837,000) of households, no people are disabled

- 29.5% (397,000) of households include one disabled member

- in the remaining 8.4% (114,000) of households, two or more people are disabled within the household

The Welsh local authorities with the highest proportion of two or more disabled people within a household were, Neath Port Talbot (10.4%), Caerphilly (10.2%), and Rhondda Cynon Taf (9.8%). Out of the top seven local authorities with the highest proportion of two or more disabled people within a household, six of them were within Wales.

Figure 3: How disability within households varied across local authorities in England and Wales, 2021

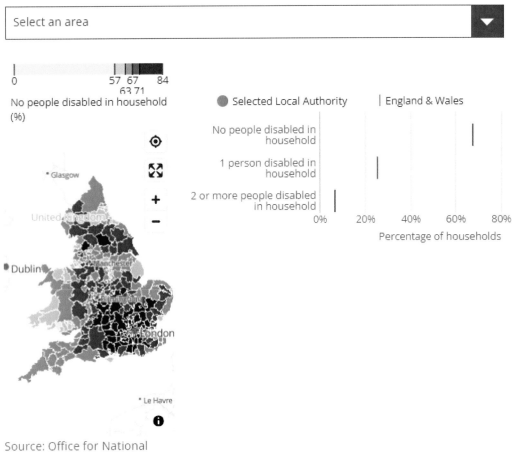

Note: This is a snapshot of an interactive image, to view the full image please go to: https://www.ons.gov.uk/peoplepopulationandcommunity/healthandsocialcare/healthandwellbeing/bulletins/disabilityenglandandwales/census2021

Notes:

1. Household level data are not age-standardised.

Download the data

.xlsx (https://www.ons.gov.uk/visualisations/dvc2218/disability_fig3/datadownload.xlsx)

5. Future publications

More detailed data and analysis on health, disability and unpaid care will be published in the coming months, alongside the release of multivariate data. Read more about our health, disability and unpaid care analysis plans (https://www.ons.gov.uk/census/aboutcensus/censusproducts/analysis/healthdisabilityandunpaidcareanalysisplans) and the release plans for Census 2021 (https://www.ons.gov.uk/census/aboutcensus/releaseplans) more generally.

6. Disability, England and Wales: data

Disability (https://www.ons.gov.uk/datasets/TS038/editions/2021/)

Dataset | Released 19 January 2023

This dataset provides Census 2021 estimates that classify usual residents in England and Wales by long-term health problems or disabilities. The estimates are as at Census Day, 21 March 2021.

Disability, age-standardised proportions (https://www.ons.gov.uk/datasets/TS038ASP/editions/2021/)

Dataset | Released 19 January 2023

This dataset provides Census 2021 estimates that classify usual residents in England and Wales by long-term health problems or disabilities. The estimates are as at Census Day, 21 March 2021. Age-standardisation allows for comparisons between populations that may contain proportions of different ages.

Number of disabled people in household (https://www.ons.gov.uk/datasets/TS040/editions/2021/)

Dataset | Released 19 January 2023

This dataset provides Census 2021 estimates that classify households in England and Wales by the number of disabled people in the household. The estimates are as at Census Day, 21 March 2021.

7. Glossary

Disability

People who assessed their day-to-day activities as limited by long-term physical or mental health conditions or illnesses are considered disabled. This definition of a disabled person meets the harmonised standard for measuring disability (https://analysisfunction.civilservice.gov.uk/policy-store/measuring-disability-for-the-equality-act-2010/) and is in line with the Equality Act (2010).

Number of disabled people in household

The number of people in a household who assessed their day-to-day activities as limited by long-term physical or mental health conditions or illnesses and are considered disabled. This definition of a disabled person meets the harmonised standard for measuring disability and is in line with the Equality Act (2010).

Usual resident

For Census 2021, a usual resident of the UK is anyone who, on Census Day, was in the UK and had stayed or intended to stay in the UK for a period of 12 months or more or had a permanent UK address and was outside the UK and intended to be outside the UK for less than 12 months.

8. Measuring the data

Age-standardised proportions

Age-standardised proportions (ASPs) allow for fairer comparison between populations over time and across geographies, as they account for differences in the population size and age structure. The 2013 European Standard Population (https://webarchive.nationalarchives.gov.uk/ukgwa/20160106020035/http://www.ons.gov.uk/ons/guide-method/user-guidance/health-and-life-events/revised-european-standard-population-2013--2013-esp-/index.html) is used to standardise proportions.

Question change

Census 2021 asked usual residents to report if they had a long-term physical or mental health condition or illness, lasting or expected to last 12 months or more, and whether it limited their day-to-day activities "a little", "a lot" or "not at all". This is set out in more detail in our Health and unpaid care question development for Census 2021 (https://www.ons.gov.uk/census/planningforcensus2021/questiondevelopment/healthandunpaidcarequestiondevelopmentforcensus2021) report.

Census 2011 asked usual residents whether their day-to-day activities were limited because of a health problem or disability which has lasted, or is expected to last, at least 12 months.

The questions differed so that we could collect data that more closely aligned with the definition of disability in the Equality Act (2010 (https://www.gov.uk/guidance/equality-act-2010-guidance)). This requires that a person has a physical or mental impairment, and that the impairment has a substantial and long-term adverse effect on a person's ability to carry out day-to-day activities.

Therefore, those reporting conditions that limited their day-to-day activities a little or a lot were classified as disabled under the Equality Act (2010). People who had no long-term physical or mental health conditions, or who had conditions that did not limit their day-to-day activities were classified as non-disabled under the Equality Act (2010).

Reference date

The census provides estimates of the characteristics of all people and households in England and Wales on Census Day, 21 March 2021. It is carried out every 10 years and gives us the most accurate estimate of all the people and households in England and Wales.

We are responsible for carrying out the census in England and Wales but will also release outputs for the UK in partnership with the Welsh Government, the National Records of Scotland (NRS) and the Northern Ireland Statistics and Research Agency (NISRA). The census in Northern Ireland was also conducted on 21 March 2021, whereas Scotland's census was moved to 20 March 2022. All UK census offices are working closely together to understand how this difference in reference dates will affect UK-wide population and housing statistics, in terms of both timing and scope.

Response rate

The person response rate (https://www.ons.gov.uk/peoplepopulationandcommunity/populationandmigration/populationestimates/methodologies/measuresshowingthequalityofcensus2021estimates#response-rates) is the number of usual residents for whom individual details were provided on a returned questionnaire, divided by the estimated usual resident population.

The person response rate for Census 2021 was 97% of the usual resident population of England and Wales, and over 88% in all local authorities. Most returns (89%) were received online. The response rate exceeded our target of 94% overall and 80% in all local authorities.

Read more about question-specific response rates at local authority level in Section 4 of our Measures showing the quality of Census 2021 estimates methodology (https://www.ons.gov.uk/peoplepopulationandcommunity/populationandmigration/populationestimates/methodologies/measuresshowingthequalityofcensus2021estimates#item-non-response-edit-and-imputation-rates).

9. Strengths and limitations

Quality considerations, along with the strengths and limitations of Census 2021 more generally, can be found in our Quality and Methodology Information (QMI) for Census 2021 (https://www.ons.gov.uk/peoplepopulationandcommunity/populationandmigration/populationestimates/methodologies/qualityandmethodologyinformationqmiforcensus2021#quality-summary). Read more about the Health, disability and unpaid care quality information for Census 2021 (https://www.ons.gov.uk/peoplepopulationandcommunity/healthandsocialcare/healthandwellbeing/methodologies/healthdisabilityandunpaidcarequalityinformationforcensus2021).

Further information on our quality assurance processes is provided in our Maximising the quality of Census 2021 population estimates report (https://www.ons.gov.uk/peoplepopulationandcommunity/populationandmigration/populationestimates/methodologies/maximisingthequalityofcensus2021populationestimates).

10. Related links

Census maps (https://www.ons.gov.uk/census/maps)

Interactive content | Updated 19 January 2023

Interactive map tool that visualises Census 2021 data on different topics down to a local authority area and neighbourhood level.

Health, disability and unpaid care quality information for Census 2021 (https://www.ons.gov.uk/peoplepopulationandcommunity/healthandsocialcare/healthandwellbeing/methodologies/healthdisabilityandunpaidcarequalityinformationforcensus2021)

Methodology | Released 19 January 2023

Known quality information affecting health, disability and unpaid care data from Census 2021 in England and Wales.

Health, disability and unpaid care variables, Census 2021 (https://www.ons.gov.uk/census/census2021dictionary/variablesbytopic/healthdisabilityandunpaidcarevariablescensus2021)

Supporting information | Released 19 January 2023

Variables and classifications used in Census 2021 data about health, disability and unpaid care.

Health, disability and unpaid care in Wales (Census 2021) (https://www.gov.wales/health-disability-and-provision-unpaid-care-wales-census-2021)

Bulletin | Released 19 January 2023

A summary by Welsh Government of Census 2021 data about health, disability and unpaid care in Wales.

How your area has changed in 10 years: Census 2021 (https://www.ons.gov.uk/peoplepopulationandcommunity/populationandmigration/populationestimates/articles/howyourareahaschangedin10yearscensus2021/2022-11-08)

Digital content article | Updated 19 January 2023

Find out how life changed for people living in different local authority areas in England and Wales.

11. Cite this statistical bulletin

Office for National Statistics (ONS), released 19 January 2023, ONS website, statistical bulletin, Disability, England and Wales: Census 2021 (https://www.ons.gov.uk/peoplepopulationandcommunity/healthandsocialcare/healthandwellbeing/bulletins/disabilityenglandandwales/census2021)

Contact details for this statistical bulletin

Beth Waddington
census.customerservices@ons.gov.uk
Telephone: +44 01329 444972

Data and analysis from Census 2021

Influenza and other respiratory viruses pilot study, Coronavirus (COVID-19) Infection Survey, UK: October 2022 to February 2023

Summary of findings from the influenza (flu) and Respiratory Syncytial Virus (RSV) pilot survey, which ran from October 2022 to February 2023, as part of the Coronavirus (COVID-19) Infection Survey (CIS). This pilot is delivered in partnership with the University of Oxford, University of Manchester, UK Health Security Agency (UKHSA) and Wellcome Trust, working with the University of Oxford and partner laboratories to collect and test samples.

Contact:
Michelle Bowen, Gillian Flower and Lina Lloyd

Release date:
27 March 2023

Table of contents

1. Main points

- The Coronavirus (COVID-19) Infection Survey (CIS) has been hugely successful at monitoring levels of COVID-19 infections and antibodies in the population; exploratory work has been conducted to understand whether other viruses that cause respiratory illness could be monitored in the same way.

- Over the course of a 20-week pilot, a total of 14,900 nose and throat samples were tested for two other respiratory viruses in addition to COVID-19.

- Over this 20-week period, 130 participants tested positive for influenza (flu) A or B, representing 0.9% of our sample (95% confidence interval: 0.7% to 1.0%), and 180 participants tested positive for Respiratory Syncytial Virus (RSV), representing 1.2% of our sample (95% confidence interval: 1.0% to 1.4%).

- Using survey samples in this way has shown how the Coronavirus (COVID-19) Infection Survey could support any future health surveillance strategy by providing early warning of levels of flu and RSV in the population, as well as providing more information on which flu strains are in circulation.

2. Overview of the pilot study

The Coronavirus (COVID-19) Infection Survey (CIS) was initiated in April 2020, in response to the immediate risks posed by the coronavirus pandemic. The survey was established to provide timely monitoring of COVID-19 infection levels across the UK, by testing nose and throat swabs taken from a representative sample of participants. These samples are tested using reverse transcriptase polymerase chain reaction (RT-PCR) (https://www.ons.gov.uk/peoplepopulationandcommunity/healthandsocialcare/healthandlifeexpectancies/articles/influenzaandotherrespiratoryvirusespilotstudycoronaviruscovid19infectionsurveyuk/october2022tofebruary2023#glossary) to detect the presence of SARS-CoV-2, the specific virus that causes COVID-19. For further information please refer to our Coronavirus (COVID-19) Infection Survey: methods and further information (https://www.ons.gov.uk/peoplepopulationandcommunity/healthandsocialcare/conditionsanddiseases/methodologies/covid19infectionsurveypilotmethodsandfurtherinformation#study-design-data-we-collect).

SARS-CoV-2 (https://www.ons.gov.uk/peoplepopulationandcommunity/healthandsocialcare/healthandlifeexpectancies/articles/influenzaandotherrespiratoryvirusespilotstudycoronaviruscovid19infectionsurveyuk/october2022tofebruary2023#glossary) is one type of virus that causes respiratory illness that can include a range of symptoms such as cough, sore throat and fever (high temperature). Influenza (flu) (https://www.ons.gov.uk/peoplepopulationandcommunity/healthandsocialcare/healthandlifeexpectancies/articles/influenzaandotherrespiratoryvirusespilotstudycoronaviruscovid19infectionsurveyuk/october2022tofebruary2023#glossary) viruses A and B also cause respiratory illness and are responsible for flu seasons in the winter months each year. Similarly, Respiratory Syncytial Virus (RSV) (https://www.ons.gov.uk/peoplepopulationandcommunity/healthandsocialcare/healthandlifeexpectancies/articles/influenzaandotherrespiratoryvirusespilotstudycoronaviruscovid19infectionsurveyuk/october2022tofebruary2023#glossary) can also cause coughs and colds in winter months. When increasing numbers of the population have these viruses it can cause pressure on our health system.

Flu cases have been historically low since the emergence of COVID-19. This is because public health measures taken to reduce the transmission of COVID-19 also reduce the spread of other viruses that cause respiratory infections like flu. For more information, see the World Health Organization's web page on influenza in the northern hemisphere, 14 October 2022 (https://www.who.int/news/item/14-10-2022-influenza-in-the-northern-hemisphere-is-back). Since these measures have been removed, many people predicted the 2022 to 2023 influenza season would be much larger and more challenging than previous years.

Our main protection from flu is vaccination. Each year vaccinations are provided based on the specific flu strains predicted to be in circulation in winter months, see the Centres for Disease Control and Prevention's Selecting Viruses for the Seasonal Influenza Vaccine web page (https://www.cdc.gov/flu/prevent/vaccine-selection.htm). Sometimes this prediction does not match the type of flu that ends up circulating, resulting in larger outbreaks of disease.

At present, most information about flu comes from people admitted to hospital. There is currently very little information about how much flu circulates in the community, particularly in people without symptoms, who may spread it without knowing.

This pilot has successfully shown that the Coronavirus (COVID-19) Infection Survey could be expanded to provide more accurate information about specific flu strains circulating within the community, and act as an early warning for the NHS.

The influenza and other respiratory viruses pilot

The pilot study was conducted from 10 October 2022 to 26 February 2023 to understand how the existing CIS could be used to monitor these additional viruses that cause respiratory illness in the community. A random selection of approximately 750 samples per week was taken from existing CIS samples (with research ethics approval) and tested for two additional viruses as well as SARS-CoV-2. These samples were processed by the Berkshire and Surrey Pathology Services (BSPS) laboratory where multiplex RT-PCR (https://www.ons.gov.uk/peoplepopulationandcommunity/healthandsocialcare/healthandlifeexpectancies/articles/influenzaandotherrespiratoryvirusespilotstudycoronaviruscovid19infectionsurveyuk/october2022tofebruary2023#glossary) testing was used to detect the presence of SARS-CoV-2, flu A and B and RSV.

We were also able to analyse test results according to demographic characteristics such as age, and whether participants reported symptoms.

Results from this exploratory work are experimental and are not considered representative of the UK population. This pilot used a relatively small number of samples, results are unweighted and do not necessarily reflect the characteristics of the UK population in general.

It should be noted that it is possible to test positive for flu after vaccination with the Live Attenuated Influenza Vaccine (LAIV), for further information regarding test accuracy refer to Section 7: Data sources and quality (https://www.ons.gov.uk/peoplepopulationandcommunity/healthandsocialcare/healthandlifeexpectancies/articles/influenzaandotherrespiratoryvirusespilotstudycoronaviruscovid19infectionsurveyuk/october2022tofebruary2023#data-sources-and-quality).

3. Experimental Results

From 10 October 2022 to 26 February 2023 a total of 14,900 samples were tested. Over this period:

- 130 participants tested positive for flu A or B, this was 0.9% of the sample (95% confidence interval: 0.7% to 1.0%)

- 180 participants tested positive for Respiratory Syncytial Virus (RSV), this was 1.2% of the sample (95% confidence interval: 1.0% to 1.4%)

- there were 12 instances where participants tested positive for more than one virus (SARS-CoV-2, flu A or B or RSV)

 Caution should be taken when interpreting these results. Estimates are unweighted and therefore cannot be considered representative of the UK population and are based on relatively low sample sizes.

For additional information including results according to age, refer to our Influenza and other respiratory viruses pilot dataset (https://www.ons.gov.uk/peoplepopulationandcommunity/healthandsocialcare/healthandlifeexpectancies/datasets/influenzaandotherrespiratoryvirusespilotstudycoronaviruscovid19infectionsurvey).

Whole genome sequencing

Samples that tested positive for flu A or B and had a sufficient amount of virus in them were sent for whole genome sequencing. This involves a detailed investigation to work out the letters that make up the genetic material of the virus in the sample. The specific strain can be identified through comparisons with the genetic sequences of known flu A or B strains.

Of the 130 participants that tested positive for flu A or B from 10 October 2022 to 26 February 2023, 50 samples underwent whole genome sequencing. Of these 50 samples, 48 samples were identified as influenza A (H3N2 or H1N1), one was influenza B and one was related to a recent vaccination with the live influenza virus. The influenza A strains identified were represented within the seasonal flu vaccine.

Symptoms

As well as testing the samples for additional respiratory viruses, we were able to link the results to questionnaire responses. Where people tested positive for flu A or B or RSV, we analysed the self-reported symptoms the participants recorded. This helps to understand asymptomatic cases and also the most common symptoms associated with each illness.

The Coronavirus (COVID-19) Infection Survey (CIS) questionnaire asks participants to select from a list of symptoms that they have been experiencing. It is important to note that not all symptoms recorded may be related to flu or RSV infection. We used the European Centre for Disease Control (ECDC) definition of influenza-like illness (ILI) (https://www.ecdc.europa.eu/en/seasonal-influenza), which allows us to analyse a defined group of symptoms out of all the symptoms reported at the time of infection. This definition defines influenza-like illness as at least one of fever, fatigue, headache or myalgia and at least one of cough, sore throat or shortness of breath. Of those in our sample who tested positive for flu A or B or RSV, we also considered the proportion who did not report any of these eight flu-like symptoms (but may or may not have reported other symptoms).

Our pilot data show that, of the 130 participants in our sample who tested positive for flu A or B:

- 56 reported symptoms under the ECDC ILI definition, representing 43.1% of the flu A or B positive cases in our sample (95% confidence interval 34.4% to 52.0%)

- 42 did not report any flu-like symptoms, representing 32.3% of the flu A or B positive cases in our sample (95% confidence interval: 24.4% to 41.1%)

Of the 180 participants in our pilot data sample who tested positive for RSV:

- 58 reported symptoms under the ECDC ILI definition, representing 32.2% of the RSV positive cases in our sample (95% confidence interval: 25.5% to 39.6%)

- 83 did not report any flu-like symptoms, representing 46.1% of the RSV positive cases in our sample (95% confidence interval: 38.7% to 53.7%)

A substantial proportion of individuals in our sample that tested positive for flu A or B or RSV did not report flu-like symptoms. These results highlight the potential insight into community transmission of viruses such as flu A or B and RSV among individuals with no or relatively few flu-like symptoms.

4. Comparing with other sources

The main existing source of information on flu and Respiratory Syncytial Virus (RSV) is the Weekly national Influenza and COVID-19 surveillance reports produced and published by the UK Health Surveillance Agency (UKHSA) (PDF, 2,989KB) (https://assets.publishing.service.gov.uk/government/uploads/system/uploads/attachment_data/file/1143318/Weekly_Flu_and_COVID-19_report_w11_v2.pdf). These reports include laboratory-confirmed influenza and coronavirus (COVID-19) cases admitted to hospital and critical care units, as well as outbreaks of respiratory infection in other settings such as care homes, prisons and schools.

Comparisons between our pilot data and the UKHSA surveillance data help us to understand how representative our pilot data is.

The trends are broadly the same between the two sources. For example, both sources show a peak in flu positivity from mid to late December 2022. The Coronavirus (COVID-19) Infection Survey (CIS) and the UKHSA weekly surveillance report test individuals in different settings, and therefore provide different results when considering the estimated proportion of individuals testing positive for flu A or B and RSV. The sample used in our pilot is also relatively small and therefore cannot be considered representative of the UK population in general.

Despite the low sample sizes in the pilot, the trends and timing are broadly similar, supporting the idea that the Coronavirus (COVID-19) Infection Survey, using a larger sample, could be used as an additional measure for flu and RSV in any future health surveillance programme.

5. Influenza and other respiratory viruses pilot data

Influenza and other respiratory viruses pilot study: Coronavirus (COVID-19) Infection Survey (https://www.ons.gov.uk/peoplepopulationandcommunity/healthandsocialcare/healthandlifeexpectancies/datasets/influenzaandotherrespiratoryvirusespilotstudycoronaviruscovid19infectionsurvey)
Dataset | Released 27 March 2023
Analysis from a Coronavirus (COVID-19) Infection Survey pilot, which tested for influenza (flu) and Respiratory Syncytial Virus (RSV) from October 2022 to February 2023.

6. Glossary

Confidence interval

A confidence interval gives an indication of the degree of uncertainty of an estimate, showing the precision of a sample estimate. The 95% confidence intervals are calculated so that if we repeated the study many times, 95% of the time the true unknown value would lie between the lower and upper confidence limits. A wider interval indicates more uncertainty in the estimate. Overlapping confidence intervals indicate that there may not be a true difference between two estimates.

Coronavirus

Coronaviruses are a family of viruses that cause disease in people and animals. They can cause the common cold or more severe diseases, such as coronavirus (COVID-19).

COVID-19

COVID-19 is the name used to refer to the disease caused by the SARS CoV-2 virus, which is a type of coronavirus. The Office for National Statistics (ONS) uses COVID-19 to mean presence of SARS-CoV-2 with or without symptoms.

Influenza (flu)

Influenza is a virus that causes the respiratory illness commonly referred to as flu. Symptoms can include cough, fever and sore throat.

Multiplex RT-PCR

Multiplex RT-PCR testing is a technique that allows the sample to be tested for multiple viruses at the same time.

Reverse Transcriptase Polymerase Chain Reaction (RT-PCR)

RT-PCR testing is an accredited technique that enables the detection of genetic material. The Coronavirus (COVID-19) Infection Survey (CIS) uses RT-PCR testing to detect the following three genes present in SARS-CoV-2:

- N (nucleocapsid) protein
- S (spike) protein
- ORF1ab

Respiratory Syncytial Virus (RSV)

Respiratory Syncytial Virus (RSV) is a virus that causes respiratory illness with symptoms that can include runny nose, cough and fever.

SARS-CoV-2

This is the scientific name given to the specific virus that causes COVID-19.

Coronavirus (COVID-19) definitions

Select a term to see its description

| Select a term | ▼ |

Note: This is an online interactive tool allowing users to select from a list of Coronavirus (COVID-19) Definitions and view their corresponding descriptions. Access to this feature is available at: *https://www.ons.gov.uk/ peoplepopulationandcommunity/healthandsocialcare/healthandlifeexpectancies/articles/ influenzaandotherrespiratoryvirusespilotstudycoronaviruscovid19infectionsurveyuk/october2022tofebruary2023*

7. Data sources and quality

Influenza and other respiratory viruses pilot sample

A small selection of Coronavirus (COVID-19) Infection Survey (CIS) participant swabs were analysed for this pilot. Approximately 750 samples per week were chosen at random, a total of 14,900 over the course of the pilot. These samples were processed at the Berkshire and Surrey Pathology Services (BSPS) laboratory.

Although samples were selected randomly, the sample is relatively small and cannot be considered representative of the UK population. Results are unweighted and do not necessarily reflect the characteristics of the UK population and therefore cannot be generalised.

Multiplex test sensitivity and specificity

An accredited multiplex Reverse Transcriptase Polymerase Chain Reaction (RT-PCR) test was used to detect the presence of SARS-CoV-2, flu A or B and RSV.

Test sensitivity measures how often the test correctly identifies those who have the virus, so a test with high sensitivity will not have many false-negative results. The ability of any test to detect the presence of virus will depend on how much virus there is in a sample. For example, someone who had flu a week ago will have lower levels of virus in their nose and throat than someone who became unwell more recently.

Test specificity measures how often the test correctly identifies those who do not have the virus, so a test with high specificity will not have many false-positive results.

Analysis on a limited number of samples suggests that sensitivity and specificity are greater than 96%.

Acknowledgements

This pilot was conducted in collaboration with colleagues at the Berkshire and Surrey Pathology Services (BSPS) laboratory:

- Muhammad Ehsaan - Lead Multiplex Scientist

- Eric Haduli - Senior Scientist

- Hugh Boothe - Laboratory Manager

- Reggie Samuel - General Manager

Whole genome sequencing was conducted in collaboration with colleagues at the University of Oxford:

- Sarah Walker

- David Eyre

- Jennifer Cane

- Nicholas Sanderson

- Sophie Barnett

- Teresa Street

8. Future developments

Coronavirus (COVID-19) Infection Survey (CIS) data collection is being paused from mid-March 2023. As the UK Health Security Agency (UKHSA) works to confirm its approach to surveillance, the Office for National Statistics (ONS) plans to work with existing participants to continue gathering valuable insight into the experiences of COVID-19, long COVID and other respiratory infections, details of which will be announced in due course. We thank our participants for their continued support.

9. Related links

The Bigger Picture: Using the COVID-19 Infection Survey to track other infections (https://blog.ons.gov.uk/2022/12/15/the-bigger-picture-using-the-covid-infection-survey-to-track-other-infections/)

Blog | Released 15 December 2022

Information on how the Coronavirus (COVID-19) Infection Survey has been used to monitor other respiratory infections in the private residential population.

Coronavirus (COVID-19) Infection Survey, UK (https://www.ons.gov.uk/peoplepopulationandcommunity/healthandsocialcare/conditionsanddiseases/bulletins/coronaviruscovid19infectionsurveypilot/latest)

Bulletin | Updated weekly

Estimates for England, Wales, Northern Ireland and Scotland. This survey is being delivered in partnership with the University of Oxford, University of Manchester, UK Health Security Agency and Wellcome Trust.

Coronavirus (COVID-19) Infection Survey, characteristics of people testing positive for COVID-19, UK (https://www.ons.gov.uk/peoplepopulationandcommunity/healthandsocialcare/conditionsanddiseases/bulletins/coronaviruscovid19infectionsurveycharacteristicsofpeopletestingpositiveforcovid19uk/latest)

Bulletin | Updated monthly

Characteristics of people testing positive for COVID-19 from the Coronavirus (COVID-19) Infection Survey, including antibody data by UK country, and region and occupation for England. Antibodies data published before 3 February 2021 are available in this series.

Coronavirus (COVID-19) Infection Survey: antibody data, UK (https://www.ons.gov.uk/peoplepopulationandcommunity/healthandsocialcare/conditionsanddiseases/bulletins/coronaviruscovid19infectionsurveyantibodyandvaccinationdatafortheuk/latest)

Bulletin | Updated monthly

Antibody data, by UK country and age, from the Coronavirus (COVID-19) Infection Survey.

Regional and sub-regional estimates of coronavirus (COVID-19) positivity over time, UK: 12 January 2023 (https://www.ons.gov.uk/peoplepopulationandcommunity/healthandsocialcare/conditionsanddiseases/articles/regionalandsubregionalestimatesofcoronaviruscovid19positivityovertimeuk12january2023/2023-01-12)

Article | Released 12 January 2023

Percentage of people testing positive for coronavirus (COVID-19) in private residential households by region and sub-region over time.

10. Cite this article

Office for National Statistics (ONS), released 27 March 2023, ONS website, statistical article, Influenza and other respiratory viruses pilot study: Coronavirus (COVID-19) Infection Survey, UK (https://www.ons.gov.uk/peoplepopulationandcommunity/healthandsocialcare/healthandlifeexpectancies/articles/influenzaandotherrespiratoryvirusespilotstudycoronaviruscovid19infectionsurveyuk/october2022tofebruary2023)

Contact details for this article

Michelle Bowen, Gillian Flower and Lina Lloyd
Health.data@ons.gov.uk
Telephone: +44 1633 560499

Office for
National Statistics

Data and analysis from Census 2021

Opinions and Lifestyle Survey QMI

Quality and Methodology Information for the Opinions and Lifestyle Survey (OPN), including strengths and limitations, recent improvements and quality characteristics.

Contact:
omnibus@ons.gov.uk

Last revised:
22 June 2023

Table of contents

1. Output information

- Survey name: Opinions and Lifestyle Survey (OPN)

- Frequency: Fortnightly

- How compiled: Cross-sectional sample survey

- Geographic coverage: Great Britain

- Sample size: Currently approximately 2,000 to 2,500 individuals per fortnightly period achieved

- Last revised: 29 April 2022

2. About this Quality and Methodology Information report

This quality and methodology information report contains information on the quality characteristics of the data (including the European Statistical System's five dimensions of quality) as well as the methods used to create it.

The information in this report will help you to:

- understand the strengths and limitations of the data
- learn about existing uses and users of the data
- understand the methods used to create the data
- help you to decide suitable uses for the data
- reduce the risk of misusing data

3. Important points

- From 20 March 2020 the Opinions and Lifestyle Survey (OPN) became weekly, to understand how the coronavirus (COVID-19) pandemic is affecting life in Great Britain; from 25 August 2021, as we moved to a period where COVID-19 restrictions had been lifted across Great Britain, the OPN covered roughly fortnightly periods with an issued sample size of around 5,000 adults in each period to help ensure the survey remained sustainable.

- The OPN currently covers topics relating to health, including how the coronavirus (COVID-19) pandemic is affecting households and individuals in Great Britain; it also and a range of other topics such as experiences regarding cost of living and shortages of goods; topics can be sponsored by other government departments.

- Around 5,000 adults are contacted in every period, with the achieved sample for the OPN currently approximately 2,000 to 2,500 individuals per week.

- Data collection is conducted by an online self-completion questionnaire; telephone interviews are available if requested by a respondent, however the predominant mode of collection is online.

- Estimates (including associated confidence intervals) from the OPN, are currently published by the ONS on a fortnightly basis (https://www.ons.gov.uk/releases/publicopinionsandsocialtrendsgreatbritain30marchto24april2022); this includes breakdowns by age and sex.

- OPN anonymised datasets are made available via the ONS' Secure Research Service (SRS) (https://www.ons.gov.uk/aboutus/whatwedo/statistics/requestingstatistics/approvedresearcherscheme/); anonymised data are also made available to sponsors of survey questions on the OPN; the data are available, without charge, to registered accredited researchers.

4. Quality summary

Overview

This report relates to the Opinions and Lifestyle Survey (OPN), which collects data from individuals (aged 16 years or older) in Great Britain.

Uses and users

From March 2020, the OPN was adapted to become a weekly survey used to collect data on the impact of the coronavirus pandemic on day-to-day life in Great Britain. As we have moved to a period where restrictions have been lifted across Great Britain, the OPN moved to a fortnightly data collection from 25 August 2021 onwards. It covers a variety of additional topics such as people's experiences regarding cost of living and shortages of goods, alongside measuring the impact of the coronavirus (COVID 19) pandemic.

The questionnaire collects timely data for research and policy analysis. OPN anonymised datasets are made available via the Office for National Statistics' (ONS') Secure Research Service (SRS) (https://www.ons.gov.uk/aboutus/whatwedo/statistics/requestingstatistics/approvedresearcherscheme/). The data are available, without charge, to registered accredited researchers.

Data and estimates are published on the ONS website, with estimates also shared with Government Departments.

Between March 2020 and March 2022, the ONS published a regular bulletin to monitor the social impacts of coronavirus throughout the pandemic. Since April 2022, the ONS have produced a fortnightly bulletin on Public Opinions and Social Trends using OPN data on a variety of topics including the continued impact of the coronavirus pandemic, cost of living and shortages of goods.

Data from the OPN also form part of other regularly updated publications from the ONS including:

- Weekly coronavirus round up (https://www.ons.gov.uk/peoplepopulationandcommunity/healthandsocialcare/conditionsanddiseases/articles/coronaviruscovid19roundup/2020-03-26) - a collection of short summaries of the latest data related to the coronavirus pandemic
- Coronavirus latest insights dashboard (https://www.ons.gov.uk/peoplepopulationandcommunity/healthandsocialcare/conditionsanddiseases/articles/coronaviruscovid19/latestinsights) - an interactive tool that brings together data about the coronavirus pandemic

Data and estimates are also shared with the Cabinet Office (CO) as well as other government departments. This is to provide indicators to inform policy, and to evaluate existing policies and their effectiveness at driving social and behavioural change.

Strengths and limitations

The main strengths of the OPN include:

- it allows for a very quick turnaround of data: the OPN currently collects data fortnightly, over a twelve-day period, with estimates and reference tables published on the ONS website within five days of survey completion.
- it meets data needs: the questionnaire is developed with customer consultation and design expertise is applied in the development stages
- it is flexible and responsive, allowing new questions to be included at a fast pace
- it meets users' sampling needs: questions can be run for multiple weeks, with the data combined to increase the sample size for examining small sub-groups of the population
- its questions are straightforward and directed at the majority of the population, however it is also possible to include questions only relevant for sub-samples

- robust methods are adopted for the survey's sampling and weighting strategies to limit the impact of bias
- it is accurate and reliable; the questionnaire is rigorously tested and the data is quality assured

The main limitations of the OPN include:

- in-depth probing of topic modules is not possible due to the length of the questionnaire

Recent updates

To understand how the coronavirus (COVID-19) pandemic was affecting life in Great Britain, the ONS adapted the monthly OPN survey to a weekly survey. The weekly survey was created to collect timely information on people's experiences and opinions related to the pandemic. Each week, some of the survey questions change to reflect changing circumstances and priorities during the pandemic.

From 25 August 2021 onwards, the OPN moved to a fortnightly period with a sample size of around 5,000 households in each period.

The survey covers residents of Great Britain who are aged 16 years and over.

Like the OPN prior and during the coronavirus pandemic, the OPN continues to be primarily collected through a self-completion online questionnaire. However, some responses (around 1% on average) have been collected with the help of telephone interviewers, for example when respondents indicate they are unable to complete the online survey themselves.

When weekly data collection started on 20 March 2020, the achieved sample was approximately 1,500 respondents per week. To allow for more granular analysis, the sample in England was boosted from 21 October 2020, achieving an overall response of approximately 4,000 to 4,500 per week.

From 25 August 2021 to 29 March 2022 , the OPN covered roughly fortnightly periods with the sample size reduced to around 5,000 households in each period, achieving an overall response of approximately 3,000 to 3,500 per period.

From 30 March 2022 onwards, the OPN design was updated to reflect a more sustainable survey design. These changes included:

- shortening the survey - to reduce the burden on the respondent, the average length to the survey was cut to around 25 minutes
- removing incentives for respondents - this reflected ongoing funding for the survey

At present, the overall response is approximately 2,000 to 2,500 adults per period.

The OPN before the coronavirus pandemic

Prior to the changes to the OPN survey during the coronavirus pandemic, there had been on-going improvements to the OPN. In recent years, work has been undertaken to change the design of the OPN from a face-to-face survey to a mixed mode design (online first with telephone follow-up). Mixed mode collection allows respondents to complete the survey more flexibly and provides a more cost-effective service for customers.

The first phase of transformation was completed in April 2018 when the OPN moved from "face to face" to "telephone" data collection. This phase of transformation included a questionnaire redesign. Specialist research, design and testing has been conducted to inform the transformation of the survey. Three pilot tests were conducted to understand the impact of changing mode and sample frame on data quality, sample representativeness and bias. Findings demonstrated minimal impact on most of the data. Where some differences were found, these were likely due to the redesigned question wording, which was optimised for telephone collection. For more information on the pilots and findings, please see the Opinions and Lifestyle Survey: mixed mode pilot analysis (https://www.ons.gov.uk/aboutus/whatwedo/paidservices/opinions/opinionsandlifestylesurveymixedmodepilotanalysis) article.

The second phase of transformation was completed in November 2019 with the move from telephone only to mixed mode collection. OPN data are collected using an online self-completion questionnaire with telephone interview available if required.

5. Quality characteristics of the Opinions and Lifestyle Survey (OPN)

This section provides a range of information that describes the quality and characteristics of the survey.

Relevance

(The degree to which the survey meets users' needs.)

The survey is currently a fortnightly survey with a focus on collecting information on health, including the impact of the coronavirus (COVID-19) pandemic on households and individuals in Great Britain, as well as a range of other topics such as people's experiences regarding cost of living and shortages of goods. The questions are primarily requested by government departments, as well as by universities and charities.

The Opinions and Lifestyle Survey (OPN) provides rapid answers to questions of immediate policy interest, helping to measure public awareness of new policies.

Topics that have been requested include:

- physical and mental health measures
- well-being
- loneliness
- experiences of crime
- attitudes to climate change
- public understanding of government publicity and information campaigns related to the coronavirus pandemic
- whether people are adhering to the latest guidance relating to the coronavirus pandemic
- attitudes to vaccines and mass testing
- how the pandemic has affected people's work and education

Accuracy and reliability

(The degree of closeness between an estimate and the true value.)

The total error in a survey estimate is made up of two types: sampling error and non-sampling error.

Sampling error

The OPN is a sample survey, so estimates are subject to sampling variability. Sampling variability is dependent on several factors, including:

- the size of the sample
- the effects of the sampling method
- the effects of weighting

Non-sampling error

The main sources of non-sampling error are:

- frame under-coverage
- non-response
- response errors (such as misleading questions or interviewer bias)

- errors when imputing or processing data

To minimise the effects of non-sampling errors, the questionnaire is carefully designed and tested, several attempts are made to contact respondents and extensive quality control procedures are used throughout. Weighting is also used to compensate for non-response and frame under-coverage.

Coherence and comparability

(Coherence is the degree to which data that are derived from different sources or methods, but refer to the same topic, are similar. Comparability is the degree to which data can be compared over time and domain, for example, geographic level.)

The demographic data collected and used on the OPN meet harmonised standards (https://analysisfunction.civilservice.gov.uk/government-statistical-service-and-statistician-group/gss-support/gss-harmonisation-support/harmonised-standards-and-guidance/) (across Government Statistical Service (GSS) surveys). The questions used on the survey follow the available GSS harmonisation guidance for collecting data about the impact of the coronavirus (COVID-19) (https://gss.civilservice.gov.uk/policy-store/coronavirus-covid-19-harmonisation-guidance/).

In November 2019, the OPN moved to mixed mode collection. This means that OPN data are collected using an online self-completion questionnaire. Alternatively, if required, the interview is conducted by telephone. Three pilot tests were conducted to understand the impact of changing mode and sample frame on data quality, sample representativeness and bias. For more information on the pilots and findings, please see the Opinions and Lifestyle Survey: mixed mode pilot analysis (https://www.ons.gov.uk/aboutus/whatwedo/paidservices/opinions/opinionsandlifestylesurveymixedmodepilotanalysis) article.

During the coronavirus (COVID-19) pandemic, the Office for National Statistics has published estimates of personal well-being using both the Annual Population Survey (APS) and the OPN. A technical paper (https://www.ons.gov.uk/releases/quarterlyestimatesofpersonalwellbeingintheukapril2011toseptember2020) considers the impact that the pandemic has had on data collection, to what extent this has influenced estimates of personal well-being and reviews the comparability of these estimates.

Accessibility and clarity

(Accessibility is the ease with which users can access the data, also reflecting the format in which the data are available and the availability of supporting information. Clarity refers to the quality and sufficiency of the release details, illustrations and accompanying advice.)

Anonymised data are sent to ONS' Secure Research Service (SRS) (https://www.ons.gov.uk/aboutus/whatwedo/statistics/requestingstatistics/approvedresearcherscheme/). Data are added on a fortnightly basis. The data are available, without charge, to registered accredited researchers.

Timeliness and punctuality

(Timeliness refers to the lapse of time between data collection and data delivery. Punctuality refers to the gap between planned and actual data delivery dates.)

The OPN currently collects data fortnightly, excluding certain national holidays, such as Christmas. The on-line data collection period is twelve days, with questionnaire content agreed approximately one week before data collection commencing. After the data collection period, the data are cleaned, weighted, and analysed. Anonymised data is sent to government departments who have an agreement to access the survey data, usually approximately five days after the data collection period. Data is also currently published on the ONS website, in the form of aggregated published tables (https://www.ons.gov.uk/peoplepopulationandcommunity/healthandsocialcare/healthandwellbeing/datasets/coronavirusandthesocialimpactsongreatbritaindata).

For more details on related releases, the GOV.UK release calendar (https://www.gov.uk/government/statistics/announcements) is available online and provides advance notice of release dates.

Concepts and definitions (including list of changes to definitions)

(Concepts and definitions describe the legislation governing the output, and a description of the classifications used in the output.)

Proxy response

The OPN is different from other ONS social surveys in that it does not, generally, collect proxy responses (responses from another adult on behalf of the selected adult). This is because a large proportion of questions asked on the survey are opinions questions. These are unsuitable for proxy collection due to their subjective nature, which if collected would reduce the accuracy and quality of the data through adding missing or inaccurate responses.

There are some exceptions to this where it is appropriate to collect a proxy response. These questions generally reflect the experiences of the household rather than the individual. For example, questions on household income.

Why you can trust our data

The ONS is the UK's largest independent producer of statistics and its National Statistics Institute. The Data Policies and Information Charter (https://www.ons.gov.uk/aboutus/transparencyandgovernance/lookingafterandusingdataforpublicbenefit/policies), available on the ONS website, details how data are collected, secured and used in the publication of statistics. We treat the data that we hold with respect, keeping it secure and confidential, and we use statistical methods that are professional, ethical and transparent. More information about our data policies is available.

The OPN is carefully designed and tested, and extensive quality control procedures are used throughout.

6. Methods used to produce the Opinions and Lifestyle Survey (OPN) data

Data collection for the OPN is primarily collected through a self-completion online questionnaire. Alternatively, if required, the interview is conducted by telephone, with approximately 1% of responses being collected with the help of telephone interviewers. The population of interest is residents of Great Britain aged 16 years and older.

Sampling frame

From March 2020, respondents who have taken part in previous ONS household surveys (such as the Labour Force Survey (https://www.ons.gov.uk/employmentandlabourmarket/peopleinwork/employmentandemployeetypes/methodologies/labourforcesurveylfsqmi) and The Living Costs and Food Survey (https://www.ons.gov.uk/peoplepopulationandcommunity/personalandhouseholdfinances/expenditure/methodologies/livingcostsandfoodsurveytechnicalreportfinancialyearsendingmarch2018andmarch2019)) have been included in the sample frame for the OPN.

From September 2020 onwards, the OPN sample has been drawn from respondents to the Labour Market Survey (LMS).

The sampling frame used for the LMS is the Royal Mail's Postcode Address File (PAF) of small users. The PAF is the most comprehensive address database in the UK. It is updated daily and contains approximately 30 million addresses. The sample for the LMS covers the whole of Great Britain.

Sampling

A two-stage approach is applied to sampling. In the first stage, a sample of households is drawn from the sample frame; in the second stage, one individual from each sampled household is selected. To overcome under-representation of younger age groups in the sample taken from the LMS, younger (aged under 25 years) and older (aged over 80 years) people are oversampled.

Each fortnight, a random selection of adults are asked to take part in the OPN. Since August 2021, a sample of approximately 5,000 adults have been sampled each fortnight to take part in the OPN The selected respondent (aged 16 and older) is the only household member who is eligible to participate in the survey. Proxy interviews or responses are not permitted.

Using the LMS introduces a potential source of bias as it only includes those who have completed the LMS and not objected to re-contact. However, data collected in the previous LMS are used in the weighting process to reduce this potential bias. This is achieved by including population controls based on variables collected in the LMS. Previous data are also used to adjust for non-response bias before weighting the adjusted sampling weights to population estimates.

The use of this previous data in weighting also improves precision. This is because sampling from the LMS and the oversampling of younger age groups, makes the sampling weights in the new design more variable.

For more information please email the ONS Omnibus Service.

How we process the data

The data is validated and cleaned, variables are derived, and weights are applied. As the OPN collects information on a sample of the population, the data is weighted to enable us to make inferences from this sample to the entire population. Weighting the OPN includes calibrating by factors including region, qualification, tenure, employment, sex, and age. ONS produces and publishes estimates from the OPN together with confidence intervals for questions with sample base sizes greater than 10 cases. Where sample base for questions allows, published analysis also includes estimates broken down by various demographics (for example, age and sex).

How we quality assure and validate the data

There are quality assurance processes from the drawing of the sample and development of the questionnaire to publication of the data and estimates. These processes include:

- the accuracy of contact information in the sample is validated

- the questionnaire is tested, both by the research team and telephone operations through test scenarios

- post collection, a series of checks are conducted on the data to identify inconsistencies and invalid responses

- inconsistent or invalid responses are individually reviewed by a researcher before a decision is made about how to deal with them

- estimates are dual run and checked at multiple stages between analysis and final reference tables and publication

- the application of statistical disclosure control - suppressing estimates to avoid any disclosure of personal information.

How we disseminate the data

The ONS currently produce a fortnightly bulletin on Public opinions and social trends using OPN data on a variety of topics, having previously published a fortnightly bulletin to monitor the social impacts of coronavirus (https://www.ons.gov.uk/peoplepopulationandcommunity/healthandsocialcare/healthandwellbeing/bulletins/coronavirusandthesocialimpactsongreatbritain/previousReleases) throughout the pandemic.

Data from the OPN have also been used in many other ONS publications examining the social impacts of coronavirus, including:

- Diary of a Nation (https://www.ons.gov.uk/visualisations/dvc983/Diary_of_a_nation-20200907082746841/index.html)

- Coronavirus and depression in adults (https://www.ons.gov.uk/peoplepopulationandcommunity/wellbeing/articles/coronavirusanddepressioninadultsgreatbritain/june2020)

- Coronavirus and home schooling (https://www.ons.gov.uk/releases/coronavirusandhomeschoolingingreatbritainapriltojune2020)

- Coronavirus and the impact on caring (https://www.ons.gov.uk/peoplepopulationandcommunity/healthandsocialcare/conditionsanddiseases/articles/morepeoplehavebeenhelpingothersoutsidetheirhouseholdthroughthecoronaviruscovid19lockdown/2020-07-09)

- Coronavirus and the social impacts on disabled people in Great Britain (https://www.ons.gov.uk/peoplepopulationandcommunity/healthandsocialcare/disability/articles/coronavirusandthesocialimpactsondisabledpeopleingreatbritain/may2020)

- Impact of increased cost of living on adults across Great Britain (https://www.ons.gov.uk/peoplepopulationandcommunity/personalandhouseholdfinances/expenditure/articles/impactofincreasedcostoflivingonadultsacrossgreatbritain/november2021tomarch2022)

- Homeworking and spending during the coronavirus (COVID-19) pandemic (https://www.ons.gov.uk/employmentandlabourmarket/peopleinwork/employmentandemployeetypes/articles/homeworkingandspendingduringthecoronaviruscovid19pandemicgreatbritain/april2020tojanuary2022)

Additionally, anonymised data are sent to ONS' Secure Research Service (SRS) (https://www.ons.gov.uk/aboutus/whatwedo/statistics/requestingstatistics/approvedresearcherscheme/). Data are added on a fortnightly basis. The data are available, without charge, to registered accredited researchers.

Contact details for this methodology

omnibus@ons.gov.uk

You might also be interested in:

Lifestyle

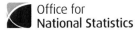

Office for
National Statistics

Opinions and Lifestyle Survey: mixed mode pilot analysis

High-level findings from pilot tests to establish the effect of transforming the Opinions and Lifestyle Survey to mixed-mode (online and telephone) data collection.

In this section

1. Summary

This article presents high-level findings from several pilot tests conducted over the last two years that were designed to establish the impact of transforming the Opinions and Lifestyle Survey (OPN). The results of the testing suggest that the transformed survey, which will be mixed-mode (online first with telephone follow-up), will continue to meet user needs by producing high-quality statistics.

Specifically, the findings from the pilot tests demonstrated that there were minimal differences in the estimates produced from the alternative designs relative to the long-standing OPN design (random probability-based sample with face-to-face data collection). A small number of significant differences were observed, however, these are likely due to improvements made to the design of certain questions. The impact of the new design on these estimates will continue to be monitored.

Allowing the option of online completion will be more flexible and convenient for respondents to take part in the survey, and the new questionnaire design will more accurately capture data required.

None of the estimates produced in any of the tests detailed in this report are official statistics and should not be used in place of any official data output from the OPN survey by the Office for National Statistics (ONS) or any stakeholder departments.

2. Background

The Census and Data Collection Transformation Programme (CDCTP) aims to rebalance the Office for National Statistics (ONS) data collection activity significantly towards wider, more integrated use of administrative and other non-survey sources, thereby reducing our reliance on large population and business surveys. While this will not eliminate a need for surveys, it does mean that the ONS's traditional approach to surveys is likely to change. The CDCTP is an important enabler of the UK Statistics Authority's Better Statistics, Better Decisions (https://www.statisticsauthority.gov.uk/wp-content/uploads/2015/12/images-betterstatisticsbetterdecisionsstrategyfor2015to202_tcm97-44175-5.pdf) strategy and some of the main features of this strategy include:

1. changing existing processes so that survey data are predominantly collected using online methods rather than using existing face-to-face interviews

2. using administrative data alongside survey data in an integrated manner to reduce the size of the residual survey samples and the number of variables that require a survey response

3. rationalising our portfolio of social surveys into an integrated framework

Within the CDCTP, the Social Survey Transformation Division is responsible for transforming the statistical design of the household survey portfolio, and all current household surveys are within scope of the programme including OPN.

3. Opinions and Lifestyle Survey (OPN) transformation

The transformation of the Opinions and Lifestyle Survey (OPN) has been taken forward in several stages and some changes have been implemented already. Details of changes made in 2018 have already been published (see the OPN methodology guide (https://www.ons.gov.uk/aboutus/whatwedo/paidservices/opinions/opinionsandlifestylesurveymethodology)).

A comprehensive programme of research and testing has been conducted to inform the transformation of the survey and this article provides an overview of this work and the main findings. This work includes several quantitative tests, which have considered the impact of mode change, redesigned questions and an alternative approach to sampling for the survey. The research aims to provide customers and stakeholders of the OPN with assurance that the quality of data collected on the survey has not and will not be undermined by the changes that are being made. The first stage of the transformation of the OPN saw the survey move from being a face-to-face interview to one that is based solely in the telephone unit. At the same time, the approach to sampling for the survey also changed and the survey is now integrated into the last wave of the Labour Force Survey (LFS) and LFS boost as a follow-up survey. This approach has been used by other surveys that ONS has conducted in the past, including the European Health Interview Survey and the Adult Education Survey.

In advance of making these changes, two pilot tests were conducted to establish the impact of this alternative methodology and main findings from these tests are presented in this article. These changes were implemented in April 2018 and since then, response to the survey has improved and the total number of achieved interviews has risen. Details of the change to OPN sampling can be found in the Appendix (https://www.ons.gov.uk/aboutus/whatwedo/paidservices/opinions/opinionsandlifestylesurveymixedmodepilotanalysis#appendix). The second stage of the transformation of the survey aims to deliver a fully mixed-mode OPN (online first with telephone follow-up of online non-responders) in November 2019. To establish the feasibility of taking a sequential approach and to understand the potential impact on data quality, a further pilot test of the mixed-mode OPN was conducted in February and March 2018. Details of this test are also outlined in this article.

It should be noted that given the nature of the survey, a multi-purpose Omnibus survey, the tests conducted were based on relatively small sample sizes. It is therefore suggested that any cross-analysis be treated with caution due to the low numbers and lack of statistical power to detect any significant differences. Collection of further data after moving to mixed-mode collection may highlight further differences not detected in the pilot tests. Monitoring of the data for mode effects will continue when the mixed-mode survey is operational and the OPN research team will work with stakeholders to help understand and address any concerns.

4. Pilot Test 1: April and May 2017

The first pilot test conducted as part of the transformation of the Opinions and Lifestyle Survey (OPN) aimed to establish the impact of changing OPN collection mode from face-to-face to telephone interviewing. This test was conducted in April and May 2017 when an issued sample of 2,010 individuals per month were approached for interview by ONS telephone interviewers. The pilot test included socio-demographic questions, as well as modules on smoking and internet access. This matched those carried on the face-to-face survey in the same months.

As well as changing mode of collection, the sample for the pilot test was drawn from the last wave of the Labour Force Survey (LFS) and LFS boost. Using this approach ensured that it was possible to pre-select the required individual for interview in the telephone unit (the face-to-face survey used a Kish grid approach).

Main findings

- Average response to Pilot Test 1 was 50% compared with 48% in the face-to-face survey over the same two months (for more information, please see the Appendix (https://www.ons.gov.uk/aboutus/whatwedo/paidservices/opinions/opinionsandlifestylesurveymixedmodepilotanalysis#appendix)).

- There was a significant difference in sex in terms of response between the two modes: on the face-to-face interview, 55% of the sample were female compared with 45% male; and on the telephone interview, the distribution was more even, as 52% of the sample were female compared with 48% male.

- The proportion of achieved response by age group was broadly similar on the telephone survey compared with the face-to-face OPN, with two exceptions: a smaller proportion of 25- to 34-year-olds responded on the telephone (10%) compared with the face-to-face interview (15%); and a greater proportion of respondents aged 60 years and over responded on the telephone (44%) compared with the face-to-face interview (37%).

- No significant differences were observed between the telephone and the face-to-face surveys in terms of response by ethnicity, housing tenure, access to a vehicle, and employment status.

- No significant differences were observed between the telephone and face-to-face surveys in terms of smoking status, and for e-cigarette usage overall.

- No significant differences were found between the telephone and face-to-face surveys for the main internet access variables.

All variables and demographic breakdowns used in the significance testing (https://www.ons.gov.uk/aboutus/whatwedo/paidservices/opinions/opinionsandlifestylesurveymixedmodepilotanalysis#appendix) can be found in the results table (https://www.ons.gov.uk/file?uri=/aboutus/whatwedo/paidservices/opinions/opinionsandlifestylesurveymixedmodepilotanalysis/variablesanalysedandsignificantdifferencesv2.xlsx).

Although the achieved age distributions showed statistically significant differences, the weighting of the dataset to population estimates helps to remove any potential bias that could result from this. In addition, accepting that the size of this pilot test was relatively small, there was no evidence of mode effects on the main smoking and internet access estimates.

5. Pilot Test 2: October and November 2017

Following on from the first pilot test, work was progressed to optimise the questionnaire for mixed-mode data collection. Kantar Public was commissioned to redesign several modules of the Opinions and Lifestyle Survey (OPN) face-to-face questionnaire for both online and telephone collection. Further information on the redesign of the questionnaire can be found in the Appendix (https://www.ons.gov.uk/aboutus/whatwedo/paidservices/opinions/opinionsandlifestylesurveymixedmodepilotanalysis#appendix).

A second pilot test was conducted in October and November 2017. This test again aimed to understand any mode effects when moving data collection from face-to-face to telephone collection but this time using the redesigned telephone questionnaire. As per the earlier test, a sample of 2,010 individuals per month was drawn from the last wave of the Labour Force Survey (LFS) and LFS boost and respondent data were compared with face-to-face data collected over the same period. The focus of the analysis was on socio-demographic, smoking and internet usage variables.

Main findings

- Average response on Pilot Test 2 was 57% on the telephone survey compared with 52% on the face-to-face survey (for more information, please see the Appendix (https://www.ons.gov.uk/aboutus/whatwedo/paidservices/opinions/opinionsandlifestylesurveymixedmodepilotanalysis#appendix)).

- Similar to Pilot Test 1, there was a significant difference in sex in terms of response between the two modes: on the face-to-face interview, 57% of the sample were female compared with 43% male; and on the telephone interview, the distribution was more even, as 52% of the sample were female compared with 48% male.

- The proportion of achieved responses by age group was broadly similar on the telephone and face-to-face surveys, except for 25- to 34-year-olds (fewer responded via the telephone) and those aged 60 years and over (more responded via the telephone).

- In contrast with Pilot Test 1, significant differences in response were observed for some categories of ethnicity: a significantly greater proportion of respondents to the telephone interview reported being White British (85.8%) compared with respondents on the face-to-face interview (77.9%); and a significantly smaller proportion of respondents to the telephone interview reported being African (0.6%) compared with the face-to-face interview (2.7%).

- In terms of housing tenure, a greater proportion of respondents on the face-to-face interview reported living rent free (2.9%) compared with the telephone interview (0.9%).

- Differences were observed in cigarette consumption at the weekend and on weekdays; significantly more respondents to the telephone interview aged 16 to 44 years reported smoking fewer than 10 cigarettes at the weekend (62.9%) compared with respondents to the face-to-face interview in the same age group (36.5%).

- The reverse pattern was observed in the same age group (aged 16 to 44 years) in terms of smoking 20 or more cigarettes on the weekend (9.0% on the telephone compared with 25.9% on the face-to-face interview).

- For weekdays, significantly more respondents aged 45 years and over reported smoking fewer than 10 cigarettes in the face-to-face interview (44.4%) compared with respondents in the same age bracket on the telephone interview (25.6%).

- In terms of e-cigarette usage, while there was no significant difference between modes in terms of current use, a significantly lower proportion of respondents reported having used one in the past on the telephone interview compared with the face-to-face interview.

- No significant differences were found between the telephone and face-to-face surveys for the main internet access variables.

All variables and demographic breakdowns used in the significance testing (https://www.ons.gov.uk/aboutus/whatwedo/paidservices/opinions/opinionsandlifestylesurveymixedmodepilotanalysis#appendix) can be found in the results tables (https://www.ons.gov.uk/file?uri=/aboutus/whatwedo/paidservices/opinions/opinionsandlifestylesurveymixedmodepilotanalysis/variablesanalysedandsignificantdifferencesv2.xlsx).

Although some differences were observed in some smoking estimates, these are possibly due to the changes made to the question designs (see Appendix (https://www.ons.gov.uk/aboutus/whatwedo/paidservices/opinions/opinionsandlifestylesurveymixedmodepilotanalysis#appendix)), which were accepted as being an improvement on the long-standing designs. The size of the test was also relatively small, and typically there is some volatility in smoking estimates between months. These estimates will continue to be monitored and stakeholders will be consulted on any potential impact on the time series.

Phase 1 of transformation complete

Following the successful completion of the first two pilot tests and subsequent engagement with main stakeholders, the OPN moved to a telephone mode in April 2018. The sample for the survey has been selected from the last wave of the LFS and LFS boost since then, and the redesigned questionnaire has also been implemented. Since launching in April 2018, response rates have been higher on average than achieved on the face-to-face survey in recent years.

6. Pilot Test 3: February and March 2018

The final pilot test aimed to establish any mode effects from changing to mixed-mode collection (online first with telephone follow-up of online non-responders) using the redesigned online and telephone questionnaires. This test was conducted in February and March 2018 and the sample size in each month was 2,010 individuals selected from the last wave of the Labour Force Survey (LFS) and LFS boost.

Data from these two months were compared with data collected from the telephone-only survey from April and May 2018 (for the socio-demographic and smoking variables). As the internet access module is carried on the Opinions and Lifestyle Survey (OPN) in January, February and April only, the data for these months were compared with the mixed-mode data from February and March 2018.

Main findings

- Average response on the mixed-mode pilot test was 61% compared with 57% for the telephone survey (for more information, please see the Appendix (https://www.ons.gov.uk/aboutus/whatwedo/paidservices/opinions/opinionsandlifestylesurveymixedmodepilotanalysis#appendix)).

- The proportion of achieved responses by age group was broadly similar with telephone and mixed-mode surveys, however, in contrast with the previous tests, a greater proportion of 25- to 34-year-olds responded to the mixed-mode survey.

- For all other socio-demographic variables considered, including ethnicity, housing tenure, access to a vehicle and employment status, no significant differences were found in terms of responses.

- Of the smoking variables analysed, significant differences were only found for the top-level estimates (males) for the grouped number of cigarettes smoked on weekdays; these questions will continue to be monitored with close user engagement with customers.

- No significant differences were found for e-cigarette use.

- No significant differences were found between the estimates for internet access.

All variables and demographic breakdowns used in the significance testing (https://www.ons.gov.uk/aboutus/whatwedo/paidservices/opinions/opinionsandlifestylesurveymixedmodepilotanalysis#appendix) can be found in the results tables (https://www.ons.gov.uk/file?uri=/aboutus/whatwedo/paidservices/opinions/opinionsandlifestylesurveymixedmodepilotanalysis/variablesanalysedandsignificantdifferencesv2.xlsx).

7. Conclusion

The testing conducted over the last two years as part of the transformation of the Opinions and Lifestyle Survey (OPN) has aimed to establish what (if any) impact there might be from changing main design features of the survey. All of the tests conducted were based on small sample sizes due to the nature of the survey and the estimates produced do not reflect official estimates.

Overall, the findings have demonstrated that there has been minimal impact on the data as a result of switching from face-to-face to telephone data collection, taking a different approach to sampling and redesigning some questions. Where changes have been observed they will continue to be monitored and stakeholders will be consulted.

There has been an overall improvement in response rates from the changes made to the design of the survey and the number of achieved interviews has also increased. The costs associated with data collection on the survey have also fallen. Based on the findings from Pilot Test 3 in 2018, we can expect response rates to improve further when we launch the mixed-mode OPN later in the year.

8. Appendix

Sample design and weighting

The Opinions and Lifestyle Survey (OPN) was initially conducted using face-to-face interviewing with a sample drawn from the Royal Mail's postcode address file (PAF) and a Kish grid approach to select an individual. A mixed-mode collection requires telephone numbers for potential respondents, therefore, the new design involves a move to the Labour Force Survey (LFS) wave 5 or the local LFS boost as the sample frame. In the last wave of the LFS and LFS boost, respondents are made aware that they may be contacted for future research. The new OPN sampling frame includes all individuals who have not objected to future research.

To ensure that the achieved age distribution in the sample selected from this frame is not too dissimilar from that achieved in the face-to-face sample, certain age groups are over- and under-sampled.

The sample design maintains a two-stage approach, with selection of a sample of households followed by selection of one individual from each sampled household. Control for any selection bias introduced from the change in sampling frame and non-response is managed through a two-stage weighting method. A model-based approach (logistic regression) is applied to the OPN data (from April 2018 onwards) for non-response adjustment using information from LFS data (based on characteristics such as region, age, sex, tenure and economic status). Then calibration factors are computed to ensure that the cases gross up to the Office for National Statistics (ONS) population totals of age group by sex and Government Office Region, as well as LFS estimates for tenure, National Statistics Socio-economic Classification, economic activity and smoking.

For further information on OPN methodology, please see the OPN methodology guide (https://www.ons.gov.uk/aboutus/whatwedo/paidservices/opinions/opinionsandlifestylesurveymethodology).

Questionnaire transformation

The OPN well-being, smoking and internet access face-to-face questions were redesigned by Kantar Public for telephone and online data collection. The project included a period of gathering data requirements from the stakeholders who commission the questions.

Kantar Public completed a desk review of the questions and proposed amendments to test. They conducted an office pilot for initial feedback before completing several rounds of cognitive and usability testing to develop the final question set. Kantar Public met with the ONS after each round to go over the findings and come to an agreement on changes required for the next iteration, contacting stakeholders for clarification on data needs when required.

As well as optimising for the mode, the questions were designed to be more relevant for users and more accurately collect the data the clients required, in line with a set of design principles agreed between the ONS and Kantar Public. This included replacing outdated terminology with more current language and breaking down questions to be more manageable.

Mode effect analysis

A statistical test at 5% level of significance was applied to identify significant mode effects. As multiple tests were applied, a Bonferroni correction for multiple comparisons tests was used to reduce the risk of type one error. A critical value was set and any test statistic whose absolute value exceeded this critical value was considered as a significant mode effect.

For Pilot Test 3, a chi square test was also run on some variables, for example, frequency of internet use, to investigate whether there was a significant difference in distribution of responses by category. The variables and demographic breakdowns used in the analysis can be found in the results tables (https://www.ons.gov.uk/file?uri=/aboutus/whatwedo/paidservices/opinions/opinionsandlifestylesurveymixedmodepilotanalysis/variablesanalysedandsignificantdifferencesv2.xlsx).

Response rates

Table 1 presents response rates for the three pilot tests.

Table 1: Response rates to the pilot tests, Great Britain, April and May 2017, October and November 2017, and February and March 2018

		Test One (April May 2017)				Test Two (October November 2017)				Test Three (February March 2018)		
April Face-to-Face	May Face-to-Face	April Telephone	May Telephone	Oct Face-to-Face	Nov Face-to-Face	Oct Telephone	Nov Telephone	April[1] Telephone	May[1] Telephone	Feb Mixed mode	March Mixed mode
46.9	50	50.1[2]	50.1[2]	51	53	56.3	57	54.7	59.1	61.3	60.3
849	929	1008	1007	927	958	1131	1145	1099	1188	1233	1213

Source: Office for National Statistics

Notes

1. Telephone collection for business as usual started in April 2018.

2. During test one the number of collection hours used was below the number allocated and interviewing was only completed to achieve the minimum 50% response rate. This was addressed for test two.

Differences between face-to-face and redesigned telephone questions (Pilot Test 2)

The differences found for the ethnicity question in test two may be due to the change made to the showcard face-to-face question to make it suitable for telephone data collection. As such, the ethnicity derivation used to compare estimates across modes was not optimised for the comparison. The face-to-face and redesigned telephone questions used can be found in Table 2.

The redesigned question is in two steps: respondents first identify which broad category ethnic group they belong to, and then the more detailed ethnic group category. Additionally, the original face-to-face question assumes those who report they are British are also White, and so the redesigned question collects better quality data and is more suited for purpose.

The new question format also seems to have reduced the number of "other" responses by better capturing ethnic group with the options available. However, it is also possible that this change in estimate is a result of the new sampling method. This should, therefore, be closely monitored during future mixed-mode data collection.

For the e-cigarette question and the differences found for the response category "I have used one in the past but I no longer use one" (test two), further investigation into these differences indicated that this change is likely due to the redesigned question. The redesigned telephone question used to derive the variable (to allow comparison with the face-to-face response categories) clearly distinguishes between "regularly used" and "just tried" responses. The face-to-face variable does not use "regularly" as part of its distinction (see Table 2). It is therefore possible that some respondents in the face-to-face sample were identifying as past "users" of e-cigarettes, when by definition they had only "tried" a device. This suggestion is also supported by lower face-to-face estimates for the "I have tried one in the past but I no longer use one" category compared with telephone estimates (for nearly all demographic breakdowns).

For the significant differences for smoking consumption (at the lower demographic breakdown), it is again important to note that the redesign of the question for telephone collection may have had an impact on the responses. The telephone questions used to derive this variable ask for the usual amount smoked for each day of the week, while the face-to-face questionnaire asks the usual amount smoked "at the weekend" and "on weekdays" (see Table 2). How respondents interpret or define "the weekend", for example, if this includes Friday, and/or focuses on more "social" occasions, may lead to the higher average number of cigarettes at the weekend for the face-to-face sample.

Table 2: Face-to-face and redesigned telephone questions for the Opinions and Lifestyle Survey

Face-to-Face question	Redesigned telephone question used in Pilot Test Two
Ethnicity	
Ethnicity	Ethnic[1]
To which of these groups do you belong?	What is your ethnic group? Is it…
1) English, Welsh, Scottish, Northern Irish, British	
2) Irish	1) White
3) Gypsy or Irish Traveller	2) Mixed or multiple ethnic groups
4) Any other White background	3) Asian or Asian British
5) White and Black Caribbean	4) African, Caribbean or Black British or
6) White and Black African	5) Another ethnic group, for example Chinese, Arab or any other background?
7) White and Asian	
8) Any other Mixed/Multiple Ethnic background	Ask if Ethnic = 1
9) Indian	Is your White ethnic group…
10) Pakistani	1) Welsh, Scottish, English, Northern Irish or British
11) Bangladeshi	British
12) Chinese	2) Irish
13) Any other Asian background	3) Gypsy or Irish Traveller, or
14) African	4) Another White background? (Ask to specify)
15) Caribbean	
16) Any other Black/African/Caribbean background	Ask if Ethnic = 2
17) Arab	Is your mixed or multiple ethnic group…
18) Any other Ethnic group	
	1) White and Black Caribbean,
	2) White and Black African,
	3) White and Asian, or
Refusal	4) Another mixed or multiple ethnic background? (Ask to specify)
Don't know	Ask if Ethnic = 3
	Is your Asian or Asian British ethnic group…
	1) Indian
	2) Pakistani
	3) Bangladeshi, or
	4) Another Asian background? (Ask to specify)
	Ask if Ethnic = 4
	Is your Black ethnic group…
	1) African
	2) Caribbean, or
	3) Another Black, African or Caribbean background? (Ask to specify)
	Ask if Ethnic = 5
	Is your ethnic group…
	1) Chinese
	2) Arab, or
	3) Another background? (Ask to specify)

Smoking consumption

M210_2	M210_Mon to M210_Sun
How many cigarettes a day do you usually smoke at weekends? smoke on… Please exclude electronic cigarettes.	How many cigarettes a day do you usually smoke on each day of the week? How many do you 1) Monday [Enter number] 999) Don't know 998) Prefer not to answer 2) Tuesday [Enter number] 999) Don't know 998) Prefer not to answer 3) Wednesday [Enter number] 999) Don't know 998) Prefer not to answer 4) Thursday [Enter number] 999) Don't know 998) Prefer not to answer
M210_3 How many cigarettes a day do you usually smoke on weekdays? Please exclude electronic cigarettes.	5) Friday [Enter number] 999)Don't know 998) Prefer not to answer 6) Saturday [Enter number] 999) Don't know 998) Prefer not to answer 7) Sunday [Enter number] 999) Don't know 998) Prefer not to answer

E-cigarette use

MEG_1	MEG_1a
Showcard if MEG_SelfCom <> 1 Have you ever used an electronic cigarette (e-cigarette)? 1) No, I have never used one and I will not use one in the future 2) No, I have never used one but I might use one in the future 3) Yes, I have used one in the past but I no longer use one 4) Yes, I currently use one 5) I tried one, but I did not go on to use it 6) I don't know what an electronic cigarette is (Spontaneous only)	Do you currently use… 1) E-cigarettes 2) A vaping device 3) Both 4) Or neither Ask if MEG_1a = 4 MEG_1b Have you ever regularly used or tried an e-cigarette or a vaping device? 1) Yes, I used it regularly 2) Yes, I just tried it 3) No Ask if MEG_1b = 2,3[2] MEG_1c How likely are you to use e-cigarettes or a vaping device in the future? Are you… 1) Very likely 2) Fairly likely 3) Neither likely nor unlikely 4) Fairly unlikely 5) Very unlikely

Source: Office for National Statistics

Notes:

1. Ethnicity data are collected using these redesigned questions. The data are then derived into the 18 categories used in the face-to-face question and delivered to customers on this basis.

2. An issue was identified with the routing for MEG_1c and has been corrected from June 2019. The routing displayed reflects the correct routing for MEG_1c.

3. Telephone questions may have been modified since Pilot Test 1.

Limitations

The analysis reported in this article is based on small sample sizes that are a snapshot based on two months' worth of data and therefore should be treated with some caution. Collection of further data after moving to mixed-mode collection may detect further differences not detected in the pilot studies. Monitoring effects on response rates and trends will continue post mixed-mode launch and any changes will be communicated with customers.

No explicit adjustments were applied for mode of data collection; the weighting was adjusted for selection effects but not for measurement effects.

You might also be interested in:

Opinions and Lifestyle Survey methodology

Opinions and Lifestyle Survey

Opinions and lifestyle information guide

Data and analysis from Census 2021

Adult smoking habits in the UK: 2022

Cigarette smoking habits among adults in the UK, including the proportion of people who smoke, demographic breakdowns, changes over time and use of e-cigarettes.

Contact:
Lauren Revie, David Mais

Release date:
5 September 2023

Next release:
To be announced

Table of contents

137

1. Main points

- In the UK population in 2022, 12.9% of people aged 18 years and over, or around 6.4 million people, smoked cigarettes; this is the lowest proportion of current smokers since records began in 2011 based on our estimates from the Annual Population Survey (APS).

- Of the constituent countries, the lowest proportion of current smokers was in England (12.7%); Wales, Northern Ireland and Scotland reported 14.1%, 14.0% and 13.9%, respectively.

- In the UK, 14.6% of men smoked compared with 11.2% of women; this difference has been consistent since 2011.

- People aged 25 to 34 years had the highest proportion of current smokers in the UK (16.3%); those aged 65 years and over had the lowest (8.3%) in 2022.

- In Great Britain, 8.7% of Opinions and Lifestyle Survey (OPN) respondents, or around 4.5 million adults, said they currently used an e-cigarette daily or occasionally; this is an increase from 2021 where 7.7% of people reported daily or occasional e-cigarette use.

- E-cigarette use was highest among those aged 16 to 24 years in Great Britain; the percentage of people in this age group who were daily or occasional vapers in 2022 has increased to 15.5% compared with 11.1% in 2021.

- Changes in e-cigarette usage are particularly evident in younger females, with a statistically significant increase in the proportion of women aged 16 to 24 years who were daily e-cigarette users in 2022 (6.7%), compared with 2021 (1.9%).

2. Collaboration

This publication is produced in partnership with the Office for Health Improvements and Disparities (OHID). As part of a cross-government approach to improve the coherence of statistics on tobacco and e-cigarette use, this release is published on the same day as OHID's update to their Local Tobacco Control Profiles (https://fingertips.phe.org.uk/profile/tobacco-control).

3. Smoking prevalence in the UK by sex, age and region

The Office for National Statistics (ONS) collects data on adult smoking habits
(https://www.ons.gov.uk/peoplepopulationandcommunity/healthandsocialcare/healthandlifeexpectancies/bulletins/adultsmokinghabitsingre
atbritain/previousReleases) using two surveys. The Annual Population Survey (APS)
(https://www.ons.gov.uk/employmentandlabourmarket/peopleinwork/employmentandemployeetypes/methodologies/annualpopulationsur
veyapsqmi) provides headline indicators of the number of adults aged 18 years and over who smoke in the UK, and the Opinions and
Lifestyle Survey (OPN)
(https://www.ons.gov.uk/peoplepopulationandcommunity/healthandsocialcare/healthandlifeexpectancies/methodologies/opinionsandlifesty
lesurveyqmi) collects more detailed information on smoking habits, intention to quit smoking and e-cigarette users aged 16 years and over
in Great Britain.

 **The smoking prevalence estimates from the APS for 2020 and subsequent years use an updated weighting
methodology. This is to remove the effect of the change in the method of data collection introduced at the
end of March 2020 because of the coronavirus (COVID-19) pandemic. Figures for 2020 onwards are now
comparable with previous years. Please see our methodology article**
(https://www.ons.gov.uk/peoplepopulationandcommunity/healthandsocialcare/drugusealcoholandsmoking/methodologies/adultsm
okinghabitsintheukmethodology) **for more information.**

Proportion of current smokers

Based on APS data, the proportion of current smokers in the UK in 2022 was 12.9%, or 6.4 million people. This is a decrease from 2021
(13.3% of the population), although not statistically significant
(https://www.ons.gov.uk/methodology/methodologytopicsandstatisticalconcepts/uncertaintyandhowwemeasureit#statistical-significance),
and is a 7.3 percentage point decrease in current smokers compared with 2011 (20.2% of the population).

We use the APS as the official measure of smoking prevalence in England to monitor and track progress against the Tobacco Control Plan for
England (https://www.gov.uk/government/publications/towards-a-smoke-free-generation-tobacco-control-plan-for-england) and the Khan
review (https://www.gov.uk/government/publications/the-khan-review-making-smoking-obsolete). The Tobacco Control Plan aims to reduce
smoking prevalence among adults in England to 12% or less by the end of 2022. In the UK in 2022, England had the lowest proportion of
current smokers with 12.7%, or 5.3 million people. This is a decrease in the proportion of smokers from 2021 at 13.0% (around 5.4 million
people), although not statistically significant.

In 2022, the proportion of current smokers in Wales was 14.1% (around 340,000 people), in Northern Ireland the proportion was 14.0%
(around 200,000 people), and in Scotland the proportion was 13.9% (around 590,000 people). Since 2011, there has been a statistically
significant (https://www.ons.gov.uk/methodology/methodologytopicsandstatisticalconcepts/uncertaintyandhowwemeasureit#statistical-
significance) decline in the proportion of current smokers in England, Scotland, Wales and Northern Ireland (Figure 1).

 **Official smoking prevalence estimates for Wales, Scotland and Northern Ireland should be taken from
devolved health or national surveys (see Section 6: E-cigarette use and vaping prevalence in Great Britain**
(https://www.ons.gov.uk/peoplepopulationandcommunity/healthandsocialcare/healthandlifeexpectancies/bulletins/adultsmokingha
bitsingreatbritain/2022#e-cigarette-use-and-vaping-prevalence-in-great-britain)**)**

Figure 1: Smoking prevalence continues to fall in England and Scotland in 2022, but remains constant in Wales and Northern Ireland

Proportion who were current smokers, all persons aged 18 years and over, UK, 2011 to 2022

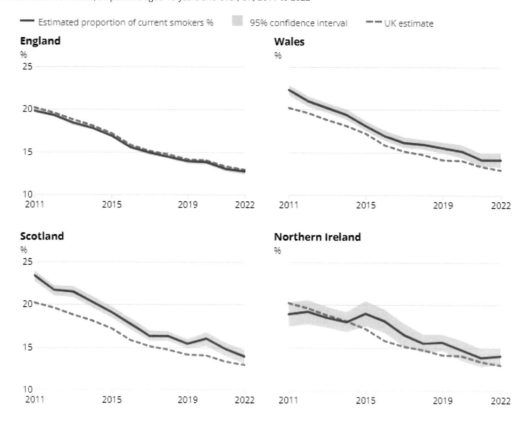

Source: Annual Population Survey from the Office for National Statistics

Notes:

1. Figures have been weighted to account for methodological changes in 2020, and to ensure estimates for 2020 onwards are comparable with estimates for previous years.

2. For Northern Ireland, the estimate over time has been more variable because of the smaller sample size.

Download the data

.xlsx (https://www.ons.gov.uk/visualisations/dvc2675/fig1/datadownload.xlsx)

In 2022, as in previous years, men were more likely to smoke than women in the UK. Across the UK, 14.6% of men (around 3.6 million) and 11.2% of women (around 2.8 million) reported being current smokers.

Those aged 25 to 34 years continued to have the highest proportion of current smokers (16.3%, around 1.4 million people), compared with any other age group. This is an increase in comparison with the same group in 2021 (15.8%, around 1.3 million people).

Those aged 65 years and over continued to have the lowest proportion of current smokers (8.3%, around 1 million people), similar to rates in 2021 (8.0%, around 950,000 people). Across time, the largest reduction in smoking prevalence has been among those aged 18 to 24 years; 25.7% of this group smoked in 2011 compared with 11.6% in 2022, a reduction of 14.1 percentage points (Figure 2).

Figure 2: People aged 25 to 34 years continued to have the highest smoking prevalence

Proportion who were current smokers, all persons by age group, UK, 2011 to 2022

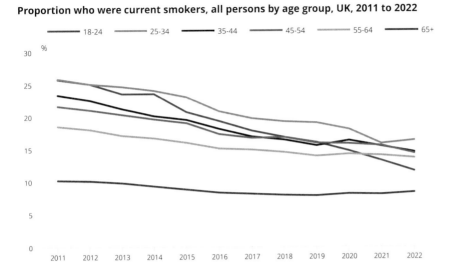

Source: Annual Population Survey from the Office for National Statistics

Local authority smoking prevalence

Since 2012, Kingston upon Hull and Blackpool have been in the 10 local authorities with the highest proportion of current smokers eight times each. In 2022, the proportion of current smokers decreased in Kingston upon Hull (18.9%) and Blackpool (18.8%), respectively (Figure 3).

In 2022, Stafford (2.9%) and Rushcliffe (4.0%) had the lowest levels of smoking prevalence in England. For more information on smoking prevalence in local and unitary authority areas by sex, see our accompanying datasets (https://www.ons.gov.uk/peoplepopulationandcommunity/healthandsocialcare/healthandlifeexpectancies/bulletins/adultsmokinghabitsingreatbritain/2019/relateddata). Local authority data for England are also available in Office for Health Improvement and Disparities (OHID) Local Tobacco Control Profiles (https://fingertips.phe.org.uk/profile/tobacco-control). This tool allows users to compare local authorities within regions and benchmark a local authority against the England or regional average.

 Smoking prevalence estimates by local authority area are subject to smaller sample sizes and therefore tend to fluctuate each year because of more statistical uncertainty. Users should therefore look at the long-term trends in smoking prevalence in authorities rather than using the estimates as an indication of year-on-year changes.

Figure 3: The proportion of current smokers by local authority of the UK

The proportion who were current smokers, all persons aged 18 years and over by local authority, UK, 2015 to 2022

Source: Annual Population Survey from the Office for National Statistics

Note: This is a snapshot of an interactive image, to view the full image please go to: https://www.ons.gov.uk/peoplepopulationandcommunity/healthandsocialcare/healthandlifeexpectancies/bulletins/adultsmokinghabitsingreatbritain/2022

Notes:

1. Smoking prevalence estimates for Buckinghamshire unitary authority are not available for 2015 to 2020.

2. Smoking prevalence estimates for North Northamptonshire and West Northamptonshire are not available for 2015 to 2021.

3. Official smoking prevalence estimates for Wales, Scotland and Northern Ireland should be taken from devolved health or national surveys.

4. Confidence intervals for local authority estimates of smoking prevalence can be found in the accompanying dataset.

Download the data

.xlsx (https://www.ons.gov.uk/visualisations/dvc2675/fig3/datadownload.xlsx)

4. Characteristics of current cigarette smokers in the UK

Smoking is known to be associated with a variety of characteristics, such as relationship status, education level and socio-economic status.

In 2022, when looking at smoking prevalence by economic activity in the UK, those who were defined as unemployed had a higher proportion of current smokers (20.5%), compared with those who were in paid employment (12.7%), and those who were economically inactive (12.7%).

Of those who were classified as being in a "routine and manual" socio-economic classification according to the National Statistics Socio-economic Classification (https://www.ons.gov.uk/methodology/classificationsandstandards/standardoccupationalclassificationsoc/soc2020/soc2020volume3thenationalstatisticssocioeconomicclassificationnssecrebasedonthesoc2020) (NS-SEC), 22.8% were current smokers, compared with 8.3% of "managerial and professional occupations". This follows the same trend since data collection began in 2014 (Figure 4). Further information on smoking prevalence by socio-economic status can be found in our Deprivation and the impact on smoking prevalence in England and Wales article (https://www.ons.gov.uk/peoplepopulationandcommunity/healthandsocialcare/drugusealcoholandsmoking/bulletins/deprivationandtheimpactonsmokingprevalenceenglandandwales/2017to2021). Data showing the odds of reporting current smoking status among adults with a routine and manual occupation based on Annual Population Survey (APS) data are also available in OHID's Local Tobacco Control Profiles (https://fingertips.phe.org.uk/profile/tobacco-control).

Figure 4: In 2022, smoking prevalence continued to be higher in routine and manual occupations than in managerial and professional occupations

The proportion who were current smokers by socio-economic status group, all persons aged 18 to 64 years, UK, 2014 to 2022

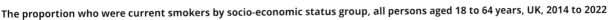

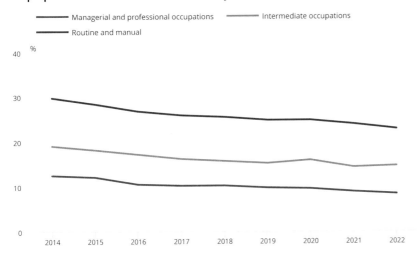

Source: Annual Population Survey for the Office for National Statistics

Notes:

1. Socio-economic class is defined using the National Statistics Socio-economic Classification (NS-SEC).

2. We have restricted the data to those aged 18 to 64 years of working age.

In 2022, 27.2% of people who had no qualifications were current smokers. This is higher than among those who reported their highest level of education as "Other qualifications" (24.5%), and those who reported GCSEs as their highest level of education (19.5%). Those who reported a degree or equivalent as their highest level of education had the lowest proportion of current smokers (6.5%) (Figure 5).

Figure 5: The highest proportion of current smokers were among those who reported they had no qualifications

The proportion who were current smokers by highest level of educational attainment, all persons aged 18 years and over, UK, 2014 to 2022

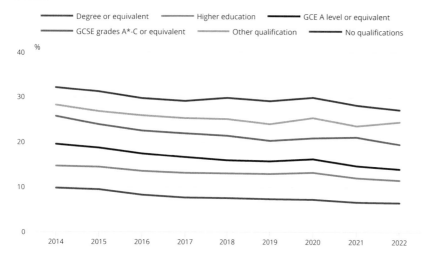

Source: Annual Population Survey from the Office for National Statistics

The accompanying dataset (https://www.ons.gov.uk/peoplepopulationandcommunity/healthandsocialcare/healthandlifeexpectancies/bulletins/adultsmokinghabitsingreatbritain/2021/relateddata) includes a wider range of data on the characteristics of cigarette smokers from the APS, including estimates by socio-economic status, relationship status, housing tenure, country of birth, ethnicity, and religion. These data for England are also available in Office for Health Improvement and Disparities Local Tobacco Control Profiles (https://fingertips.phe.org.uk/profile/tobacco-control).

5. Smoking prevalence in Great Britain

In this section, we describe data from the Opinions and Lifestyle Survey (OPN), which covers adults aged 16 years and over in Great Britain.

> ⚠ **The Opinions and Lifestyle Survey** (https://www.ons.gov.uk/peoplepopulationandcommunity/healthandsocialcare/healthandlifeexpectancies/methodologies/opinionsandlifestylesurveyqmi) **changed from an interviewer-led telephone survey to a self-completion online survey since 2020, so we recommend using caution when interpreting the movement in the trend. For more information, please see our accompanying methodology article** (https://www.ons.gov.uk/peoplepopulationandcommunity/healthandsocialcare/drugusealcoholandsmoking/methodologies/adultsmokinghabitsintheukmethodology) **and the OPN QMI** (https://www.ons.gov.uk/peoplepopulationandcommunity/healthandsocialcare/healthandlifeexpectancies/methodologies/opinionsandlifestylesurveyqmi)**.**

Current smokers

The proportion of adults aged 16 years and over who said they smoked cigarettes in Great Britain decreased significantly from 12.7% in 2021 to 11.2% in 2022, continuing the downward trend seen since 1974. This is in-line with the reduction in smoking we see in the Annual Population Survey (which covers the UK and adults aged 18 years and over).

Conversely, the proportion of people who indicated that they had previously smoked and quit increased in 2022 to 69.4%, compared with 66.9% in 2021 (Figure 6).

Figure 6: The proportion of previous cigarette smokers who have quit continued to increase

The proportion of current smokers and those who had previously smoked and have quit for all persons aged 16 years and over, Great Britain, 1974 to 2022

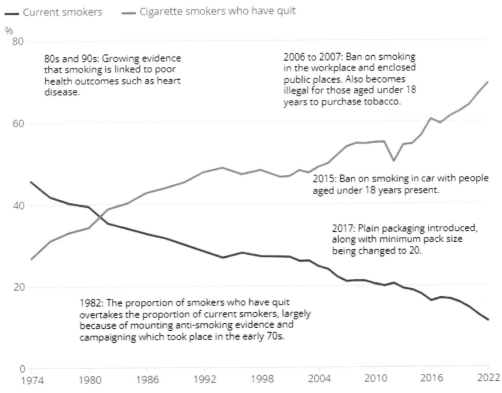

Source: Opinions and Lifestyle Survey from the Office for National Statistics

Notes:

1. The proportion of cigarette smokers who have quit is the proportion of all those who said that they have smoked cigarettes regularly who do not currently smoke.

2. From March 2020, the survey moved to weekly data collection.

3. From 25 August 2021, the survey moved to fortnightly data collection.

4. Data are weighted from 2000 onwards.

5. Data on cigarette use were collected on a two-year basis prior to 2000.

6. Information on the changes in legislation and government policy can be found on the Action on Smoking and Health (ASH) website (https://ash.org.uk/category/information-and-resources/law-guide/).

Download the data

.xlsx (https://www.ons.gov.uk/visualisations/dvc2675/fig6/datadownload.xlsx)

Of the people who currently smoked, 45.4% stated that they intended to quit smoking, with 22.0% of current smokers intending to quit within the next three months at the time of interview. When current smokers intended to quit, they also waited longer to have their first cigarette of the day after waking (Figure 7). Among those who intended to quit within the next three months, 48.0% had their first cigarette within the first hour of waking, compared with 82.3% of those not intending to quit.

Figure 7: Current smokers who intended to quit waited longer to have their first cigarette of the day

Time waited until first cigarette of the day by intention to quit, Great Britain, 2022

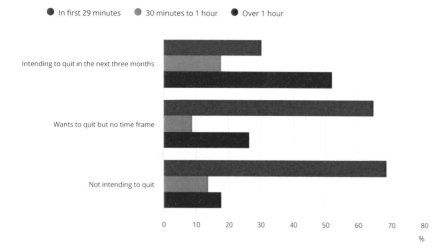

Source: Opinions and Lifestyle Survey from the Office for National Statistics

Notes:

1. The data refer to the amount of time cigarette smokers typically waited until they had their first cigarette after waking.

6. E-cigarette use and vaping prevalence in Great Britain

Data for vaping and e-cigarette use come from the Opinions and Lifestyle Survey (OPN), which covers adults aged 16 years and over in Great Britain.

In 2022, 5.2% of survey respondents reported that they were currently daily users of an e-cigarette, an increase from 4.9% in 2021 (Figure 8), although not statistically significant. A further 3.5% reported using an e-cigarette occasionally, an increase from 2.8% in 2021. This equates to around 4.5 million vapers in the population of Great Britain.

Figure 8: The proportion of current daily vapers increased in 2022 compared with 2021

Proportion of daily and occasional vapers, Great Britain, 2021 and 2022

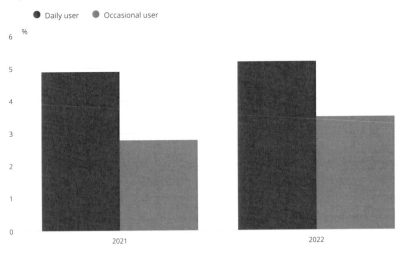

Source: Opinions and Lifestyle Survey from the Office for National Statistics

Notes:

1. The survey moved to fortnightly data collection from 25 August 2021.

In 2022, the proportion of daily and occasional vapers continued to be highest among current cigarette smokers (27.1%) and ex-cigarette smokers (16.5%). Around 2.4% of people who have never smoked reported that they were daily or occasional e-cigarette users in 2022, an increase from 1.5% in 2021. Among those who have never smoked, respondents reporting occasional e-cigarette use showed a statistically significant increase in 2022 (1.8%) compared with 2021 (0.8%).

A higher proportion of men aged 16 years and over reported vaping daily or as an occasional user (9.5%) compared with women (7.9%) in 2022.

The total proportion of young people aged 16 to 24 years who were daily or occasional vapers in 2022 increased to 15.5% compared with 11.1% in 2021 (Figure 9). Changes in e-cigarette usage are particularly evident in younger females, with a statistically significant increase in the proportion of women aged 16 to 24 years who were daily e-cigarette users in 2022 (6.7%), compared with 2021 (1.9%). This is the highest proportion of daily e-cigarette usage in this age group for females since data collection began in 2014.

Women aged 16 to 24 years who were occasional e-cigarette users also increased in 2022 to 12.2%, compared with 7.1% in 2021. Occasional e-cigarette use in younger males aged 16 to 24 years increased to 8.7% in 2022 compared with 7.9% in 2021, although this increase was not statistically significant.

Figure 9: Daily or occasional vape use was highest in people aged 16 to 24 years in 2022

Proportion of daily or occasional vapers by age, Great Britain, 2021 and 2022

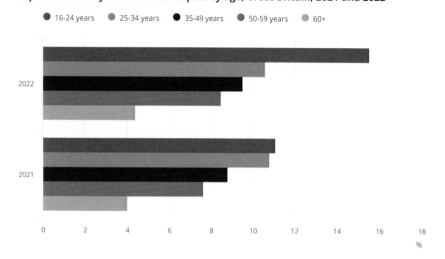

Source: Opinions and Lifestyle Survey from the Office for National Statistics

Notes:

1. The survey moved to fortnightly data collection from 25 August 2021.

7. Other UK data sources on smoking prevalence

The devolved countries of the UK each have their own health surveys that are used to provide official estimates of smoking in each country. These surveys are also used to track progress against each country's targets to reduce smoking. These are:

- the Northern Ireland Health Survey, which shows that 17% of adults smoked cigarettes in 2021 to 2022 (https://www.health-ni.gov.uk/publications/health-survey-northern-ireland-first-results-202122)

- the National Survey for Wales, which shows that 13% of adults smoked cigarettes in April 2022 to March 2023 (https://www.gov.wales/adult-lifestyle-national-survey-wales-april-2022-march-2023)

- the Scottish Health Survey, which shows that 11% of adults smoked cigarettes in 2021 (PDF, 12.7MB) (https://www.gov.scot/collections/scottish-health-survey/)

The Local Tobacco Control Profiles (https://fingertips.phe.org.uk/profile/tobacco-control) from the Office for Health Improvement and Disparities (OHID) details data on a wide range of indicators related to the smoking of cigarettes, including different measures of prevalence in adults and young people, smoking-related mortality, and the wider impacts of coronavirus (COVID-19) on health (https://analytics.phe.gov.uk/apps/covid-19-indirect-effects/). The Health Survey for England (https://digital.nhs.uk/data-and-information/publications/statistical/health-survey-for-england/) and the Smoking Toolkit Study (https://smokinginengland.info/graphs/top-line-findings) (non-Government Statistical Service) also collect data on smoking habits and e-cigarettes. NHS Digital also collect data on smoking, drinking and drug use among young people in England (https://digital.nhs.uk/data-and-information/publications/statistical/smoking-drinking-and-drug-use-among-young-people-in-england).

8. Adult smoking habits in the UK data

Smoking habits in the UK and its constituent countries
(https://www.ons.gov.uk/peoplepopulationandcommunity/healthandsocialcare/healthandlifeexpectancies/datasets/smokinghabitsinthe
ukanditsconstituentcountries)

Dataset | Released 5 September 2023

Annual data on the proportion of adults who currently smoke, the proportion of ex-smokers and proportion of those who have never
smoked, by sex and age.

E-cigarette use in Great Britain
(https://www.ons.gov.uk/peoplepopulationandcommunity/healthandsocialcare/drugusealcoholandsmoking/datasets/ecigaretteuseingre
atbritain)

Dataset | Released 5 September 2023

Annual data on the proportion of adults in Great Britain who use e-cigarettes, by different characteristics such as age, sex and cigarette
smoking status.

E-cigarette use in England
(https://www.ons.gov.uk/peoplepopulationandcommunity/healthandsocialcare/healthandlifeexpectancies/datasets/ecigaretteuseinengl
and)

Dataset | Released 5 September 2023

Annual data on the proportion of adults in England who use e-cigarettes, by different characteristics such as age, sex and cigarette
smoking status.

Adult smoking habits in Great Britain
(https://www.ons.gov.uk/peoplepopulationandcommunity/healthandsocialcare/drugusealcoholandsmoking/datasets/adultsmokinghabit
singreatbritain)

Dataset | Released 5 September 2023

Annual data on the proportion of adults in Great Britain who smoke cigarettes, cigarette consumption, the proportion who have never
smoked cigarettes and the proportion of smokers who have quit, by sex and age over time.

Adult smoking habits in England
(https://www.ons.gov.uk/peoplepopulationandcommunity/healthandsocialcare/healthandlifeexpectancies/datasets/adultsmokinghabitsi
nengland)

Dataset | Released 5 September 2023

Annual data on the proportion of adults in England who smoke cigarettes, cigarette consumption, the proportion who have never
smoked cigarettes and the proportion of smokers who have quit, by sex and age over time.

9. Glossary

Current cigarette smokers

The Annual Population Survey (APS) defines current cigarette smokers as those who said they smoke cigarettes nowadays. The Opinions and Lifestyle Survey (OPN) defines current cigarette smokers as those who said they smoked cigarettes, even if occasionally. Current cigarette smokers are provided as a proportion of those in the population.

Cigarette smokers who have quit

From the OPN, those who said they have smoked cigarettes regularly, but they do not currently smoke, are cigarette smokers who have quit. This is provided as a proportion of those who have ever smoked cigarettes regularly.

Current vapers

From the OPN, those who said they currently use e-cigarettes, a vaping device, or both, are current vapers. Current vapers are provided as a proportion of those in the population.

Survey mode

Survey mode is the method that is used to collect information from respondents. There are different types of survey mode, such as face to face, telephone, online and mixed mode.

Selection bias

Selection bias is an experimental error that occurs when the participant pool, or the subsequent data, is not representative of the target population.

Statistical significance

Significance has been determined using 95% confidence intervals (https://www.ons.gov.uk/methodology/methodologytopicsandstatisticalconcepts/uncertaintyandhowwemeasureit#confidence-interval), which provide the range of values within which we are 95% confident that the true value lies. The 95% confidence intervals for the estimates are available in the accompanying datasets (https://www.ons.gov.uk/peoplepopulationandcommunity/healthandsocialcare/healthandlifeexpectancies/bulletins/adultsmokinghabitsingreatbritain/2019/relateddata).

Economic activity

International Labour Organisation (ILO) definitions of economic activity are used. Unemployed people are those who are not currently in work but who are looking for work. The group "economically inactive" contains those who are not in work, and not looking for work; this includes retired people and students. More information regarding economic activity can be found in the Labour Force Survey user guide (https://www.ons.gov.uk/employmentandlabourmarket/peopleinwork/employmentandemployeetypes/methodologies/labourforcesurveyuserguidance).

10. Measuring the data

Annual Population Survey (APS)

The data on smoking habits in the UK come from the Annual Population Survey (APS). The survey covers residents of the UK aged 18 years and over. For further information on APS survey methodology, see our APS QMI (https://www.ons.gov.uk/employmentandlabourmarket/peopleinwork/employmentandemployeetypes/methodologies/annualpopulationsurveyapsqmi).

The change from a mixed mode to telephone-only data collection for the APS, introduced at the end of March 2020, resulted in a potentially biased sample. The change in the mode of data collection meant our smoking prevalence estimates for 2020 were not comparable with the estimates of previous years. We have updated our weighting methodology to improve comparability of our smoking prevalence estimates for 2020 and subsequent years. For more details about this update, see our Adult smoking habits in the UK methodology (https://www.ons.gov.uk/peoplepopulationandcommunity/healthandsocialcare/drugusealcoholandsmoking/methodologies/adultsmokinghabitsintheukmethodology).

Opinions and Lifestyle Survey (OPN)

Data on smoking and e-cigarette use for Great Britain for those aged 16 years and over come from the Opinions and Lifestyle Survey (OPN). In March 2020, the OPN was transformed from a monthly to weekly omnibus survey to understand how the coronavirus (COVID-19) pandemic is affecting life in Great Britain. As a result, the number of questions relating to smoking and vaping habits was greatly reduced. For more information on the OPN survey methodology, see our Opinions and Lifestyle Survey QMI (https://www.ons.gov.uk/peoplepopulationandcommunity/healthandsocialcare/healthandlifeexpectancies/methodologies/opinionsandlifestylesurveyqmi).

The analysis reported in this release used survey weights to make estimates representative of the population. Survey weights take into account non-response and attrition, as well as the distribution of population characteristics, such as sex and age, where someone lives, and socio-economic characteristics.

11. Strengths and limitations

Strengths

Robust methods are adopted for the Annual Population Survey (APS) and Opinions and Lifestyle Survey (OPN) sampling and weighting strategies to limit the impact of bias. Quality assurance procedures are undertaken throughout the analysis stages to minimise the risk of error.

The sample size of the APS is large, approximately 192,265 respondents, making it possible to generate statistics for small geographic areas. The sample size of the OPN in 2022 was approximately 64,384 respondents.

Limitations

Comparisons between periods and groups must be done with caution as estimates are provided from a sample survey; as such, confidence intervals (https://www.ons.gov.uk/methodology/methodologytopicsandstatisticalconcepts/uncertaintyandhowwemeasureit#confidence-interval) are included in the accompanying datasets (https://www.ons.gov.uk/peoplepopulationandcommunity/healthandsocialcare/healthandlifeexpectancies/bulletins/adultsmokinghabitsingreatbritain/2019/relateddata) to present the sampling variability. These should be taken into account when assessing differences between periods, as true differences may not exist.

There are differences when comparing estimates of smoking prevalence from different surveys. These differences are attributable to a range of factors, for example:

- different survey questions
- different methods of sampling
- different methods of weighting

12. Related links

Office for Health Improvement and Disparities: Local Tobacco Control Profiles (https://fingertips.phe.org.uk/profile/tobacco-control)
Web page | Updated as and when new data become available
Data on a wide range of indicators related to the smoking of cigarettes, including different measures of prevalence in adults and young people, smoking-related mortality, and the wider impacts of smoking on health.

Smoking prevalence in the UK and the impact of data collection changes: 2020 (https://www.ons.gov.uk/peoplepopulationandcommunity/healthandsocialcare/drugusealcoholandsmoking/bulletins/smokingprevalenceintheukandtheimpactofdatacollectionchanges/2020)
Bulletin | Released 7 December 2021
Impact that the coronavirus (COVID-19) pandemic has had on data collection, how this has influenced estimates of smoking prevalence and the comparability of these estimates.

13. Cite this statistical bulletin

Office for National Statistics (ONS), released 5 September 2023, ONS website, statistical bulletin, Adult smoking habits in the UK: 2022 (https://www.ons.gov.uk/peoplepopulationandcommunity/healthandsocialcare/healthandlifeexpectancies/bulletins/adultsmokinghabitsingreatbritain/2022)

Contact details for this statistical bulletin

Lauren Revie, David Mais
health.data@ons.gov.uk
Telephone: +44 1329 444110